Exciting Times
of an Ordinary
Mormon

Exciting Times
of an Ordinary
Mormon

KEITH L. HANCOCK

Copyright © 2015 Keith L. Hancock.

All rights reserved. No part of this book may be used or reproduced by any means, graphic, electronic, or mechanical, including photocopying, recording, taping or by any information storage retrieval system without the written permission of the publisher except in the case of brief quotations embodied in critical articles and reviews.

Archway Publishing books may be ordered through booksellers or by contacting:

Archway Publishing
1663 Liberty Drive
Bloomington, IN 47403
www.archwaypublishing.com
1 (888) 242-5904

Because of the dynamic nature of the Internet, any web addresses or links contained in this book may have changed since publication and may no longer be valid. The views expressed in this work are solely those of the author and do not necessarily reflect the views of the publisher, and the publisher hereby disclaims any responsibility for them.

Any people depicted in stock imagery provided by Thinkstock are models, and such images are being used for illustrative purposes only. Certain stock imagery © Thinkstock.

ISBN: 978-1-4808-1975-7 (sc)
ISBN: 978-1-4808-1976-4 (hc)
ISBN: 978-1-4808-1977-1 (e)

Library of Congress Control Number: 2015909979

Print information available on the last page.

Archway Publishing rev. date: 08/31/2015

Nov 30/22
TO MY DEAR PEN PAL COHAN
HOPE YOU WILL READ ALL OF IT
PERHAPS YOUR MOM OR DAD CAN
READ PART OF IT TO YOU
SOME IS FUN — SOME IS PRETTY HEAVY
HOPE YOU WILL ENJOY !!

MERRY
CHRISTMAS
TO ALL
OF YOU !

Portrait of Keith L. Hancock age 19 years in Argentina South America.

Acknowledgements

To: Kristie H. Fisher, my daughter, for spending many hours editing

To: John J. Fisher, my Son-in-law, for directing this work to the publisher

Cover Photo of Keith's Boots, Hat and Rope By: Keith L. Hancock

The Early Years of a Bouncing Baby Boy

WE ALL HAVE INTERESTING LIVES IF NOT EXCITING, FILLED WITH many ups and downs, good times and bad times as we grow and mature. Many of us feel that these things should be recorded for our own posterity if not for the general populous to read and to contemplate. For me, I have been recording a personal journal since 1979, going back and forth from my childhood to the present, and have found that I have lead a fairly full and interesting life in my 80-plus years sojourn.

I really have made no great and marvelous contributions to the world, but have lived a very active life, involving myself in a little of most everything that life has to offer an *Ordinary Mormon.*

My full name is Keith LaNay Hancock, named after my mother's younger brother, LaNay Christensen. I was born July 12th, 1933 in a two room house that once served as a granary on the farm five miles south of the small community of Raymond, Alberta Canada. The old wooden granary had been moved into town on a one acre garden plot, where my father had rebuilt it into a cute little house for him, Mom, me, and my two older siblings. My mother told me that being just two rooms, a kitchen and a bedroom, that she awakened in the middle of the night soon after, with the idea that the kitchen should be swapped for the area where the bedroom was, and that it needed to be done now, even at that hour. My dad never did like to make waves, and so went right to work making the change.

I was amused many years later to learn that my wife, Connie King was born three years after myself, in a house just a half a block away, with the same mid-wife attending us both. Connie tells me that when she was two or three years old, she landed many times in the irrigation ditch that ran past our garden, and thought perhaps I may have even occasionally pushed her in!

I am the second son of Alma Elisha Hancock and Mary Ella Christensen, one of six children. My father was a successful farmer in the day; however, like most of the world, was caught up in the *great depression* of the thirties. These were times of great struggle and broken dreams. After planting of grain crops, my parents told me that the grain sprouted and came up early in the spring, tall and beautiful when the lack of rain first took its toll, withering these tall full stems down to the ground. This heart break wasn't enough. The strong dry winds began to blow relentlessly day and night, causing a virtual dust bowl in the otherwise picturesque prairies replete with tall grass, and hills alive with beautiful wild flowers and luscious fruit berries of every description. Many a good farmer had to simply walk away from these beautiful farms, bidding farewell to a happy life, their chosen life profession. My father was also struggling to keep food on the table for his family and hay in the barn for the animals. For a time, he was able to chop up fence posts used to fire up the small cook stove, and of course there was still water in the well. He was also able to obtain a bit of coal oil for a dim light in the tiny house. Having an overwhelming desire to care for his beloved family, he found it necessary to take part time employment at the Knight Sugar Factory, and therefore should move into town from the farm. My mother was a great support to him, helping with all of the meaningful chores and doing her part in bringing in a little extra money. Together, while living between the small rebuilt town property and the farm, they decided to build their own new little home on the west end of the acre lot, using any and all left over materials that were in excess from the newly built Sugar Factory, spending hours shaking bits of powder from hundreds of cement sacks, finding good used boards from construction forms or from any other source available. My mom made and sold dishtowels from unwanted sugar sacks, and braved her fears while helping to shingle the roof of the new house.

As memory serves, the first of many amusing stories told to me; when as a baby in a carriage, my parents were traveling across a long prairie wagon trail returning to the farm one evening with me riding in the baby carriage and loaded in the box of their buggy. Apparently the trail was very rough and the carriage I had been placed in bounced out of their buggy, baby and all. It was after they arrived at the farmhouse a mile later, before they noted this had happened. My older sister has related to me how upset they all were, and in her four-year-old mind thought that I was gone forever, and she couldn't stop crying. The family then retraced their travels back in the dark to retrieve me, still in the baby carriage on the uneven terrain. I often joked should they have left me for the coyotes to raise, I may have turned out better!

Boyhood Escapades

IN SPITE OF THE HARD TIMES, AND THE "HUNGRY THIRTIES" STILL raging on, the new little two bedroom house was finished sufficiently for us to move in, which we did on Christmas Eve despite the fact that my father was still laid-off. However, wonder of wonders, he was called back that very day, making for a very happy Christmas, even though very slim. To celebrate, Mom allowed all three of us young children to cuddle up with her in the same bed, not withstanding the fact that there was barely enough coal to heat just one room. I remember how happy my brother and I were to receive a homemade game, the end of an apple box painted orange, with numbers and hooks on its face and some rubber canning jar rings for us to stand back and toss. Our sister was also thrilled when she thought she had another doll exactly like her existing one only to discover that mother had simply sewn some new clothes for the same doll. She was ecstatic for anything new.

The economy still bleak, my father had also accepted part time employment at the Bank of Montreal and deciding he could improve on the banking system, wrote a paper on a whole new concept of doing things to save money in this difficult economy. He then presented it to a longtime friend, Solon E. Low, who was then Provincial Treasurer for the Province of Alberta. Mr. Low read and approved of these suggestions and prevailed upon my dad to come to Edmonton to help reform banking and take part in forming the now very successful Alberta Treasury

Branch. As this was working well for all concerned and moving along nicely, the Government offered my father an additional position, that of a Pension Inspector. This entailed traveling through and around the Province, mostly farm to farm, checking with seniors on their pensions, helping fill out forms, seeing that their needs were being met, and then typing and sending in reports to the Agency in charge. As his travels many times meant being away from home for a week at a time, he found it to be a great idea to take turns taking my brother Cal and me with him in summer time. It proved to be fun for us and certainly kept us from getting into a lot of mischief together, and out of Mom's hair. On some occasions, he did take us both on the same trip, not good, because we managed different types of antics. One time while stopped at a farm, we discovered a big iron type of steering wheel on a piece of machinery and thought it would make for a great steering wheel on a bobsled. We tucked it safely under the front seat of the car, but hadn't counted on it rattling around, which it did a few miles down the road when dad heard something strange and stopped to check it out; the wheel, how on earth did that get there? Well we were in big trouble, and had to turn back and apologize to the farmer who laughed and said we could have it as he no longer used that machine. We were so relieved but not off the hook with Dad, having to take the extra time to return to the farm for our misdemeanor was no joke for him.

My father earned a good living at this job and did extra well by turning his car into a sleeping, eating and working area, thus saving the expense money he was paid. He had figured out a way to drop the back seat, using the trunk for part of his bed. He also typed his reports on a portable typewriter, and ate his meals in the car. Dad said that doing this was better than his salary.

My father's work continued going well, and the family were quite content and now getting used to living in the big city of Edmonton, thus allowing us to move to a nicer and much larger two story home close to an area near the North Saskatchewan River, spanned by the renowned *High Level Bridge*. We loved it and considered it was made just for us; indeed a boy's paradise. The river made a deep cut through the city being heavily treed on both sides, and to a young boy almost seemed mountainous. My brother Cal, two years older than myself, and I were best of friends and spent many hours at play in the trees and river bottom, encountering many homeless men whom we considered to be *tramps*, which was just another sign of the times but as I think about it now, they were probably mostly ex-military guys out of work with little means of support. They seemed harmless enough in those days and our parents never seemed to be concerned over our safety. In fact it was not uncommon for these men to stop by someone's home for a meal or a little handout of a sort.

In summer we built hideouts and trails, climbed trees and rolled used tires to the middle of the High Level Bridge, threw them over and watched 'til they got smaller and smaller before splashing in the water. In winter we built bobsleds, two small sleds joined together with a long plank, the front sled attached with a fifth wheel type of unit so that it could be steered as we went whooping down the trails over deep snow, dodging in and around trees narrowly missing them. One day I decided it would be fun to roll off the sled while traveling fast. As I did, I struck my head on a tree, rendering me unconscious for a short time. To ease the pain, I thought more of being afraid of what my parents would think of my stupidity than of my hurting head. Another one of our many capers was that of building a hideout behind the garage. However that required a bit of lumber of which we availed ourselves by borrowing a few boards here and there from houses that were being constructed in the neighborhood. Somehow we didn't get caught, but then a few boards didn't seem to be much of an item at that time. Along with building a hideout, we also built pigeon lofts and rabbit pens; there being a lot of pigeon or rabbit swiping back and forth between neighborhood kids. It seemed like we were in a lot of not so friendly fights, but all fun now that I look back on it.

Church functions were a big item for our family, being a very small congregation, we were very close as a community, and met together often. I remember it being a homey atmosphere where everyone knew everyone and feeling very secure and cared for.

The Latter-day Saint (Mormon) population, although very prominent in the city of Edmonton, was not large and at that time did not own their own building in which to hold meetings. We therefore rented facilities from other establishments, such as the Elks Hall. This worked out well for our Sunday services and some weekday functions.

The norm in our Church is for young people to be baptized at the age of eight years. This was done by the process of immersion in a baptismal font, which of course, we lacked in our rented facility. I arrived at the age of eight and was to be baptized. An alternate font was located in a church building owned by the Baptist Congregation! Although baptized at the Baptist church, the sacred ordinance was done by one in authority from our own Mormon sect, a Brother Fred Smith who was the Branch Mission Leader at the time. I don't remember a lot more of this occasion, but I do remember feeling like I was much closer to being an adult and more ready to participate in big people things.

Many of the adult members of our church were prominent Government officials or Government employees and seemed to have a lot of fun times being together for Sunday night visits and snacks. Cal and I sneaked out of bed many times to listen to the talk and laughter or sneak food.

One of the most embarrassing times of my life, being somewhat religious and probably the only Mormon in my school class, came one morning as the prayer which was the beginning of every school day at that time was being offered. I held up my hand after the prayer and said to the teacher, "Alan didn't close his eyes during prayer." Of course the teacher said "How do you know?" And then the laughter began. Well that taught me a valuable lesson that I shall never forget. I believe that I have been rather a *smart aleck* ever since.

We lived in the city of Edmonton for five years with many experiences which took place for a young boy. Among other things, I started my first grade in school there and became well acquainted with life outside of being mostly raised on a farm and later in a very small community. I enjoyed both and still do, but mostly the peace and security of our little town of four thousand.

While living in Edmonton, we made many trips for visits and holidays to Raymond where my paternal grandparents Charles Edward and Celia Mae Hancock lived on a dairy farm.

Our travels back to Raymond every summer, with the occasional winter trip, was always a fun adventure for me. I remember vividly falling asleep on one trip. When I awoke, everyone in the car was laughing about someone in a car that had passed by them. I don't even remember what it was about, however, I do remember being quite upset with myself that I had been sleeping and therefore missed the action. I then made a vow with myself that such a situation would never happen again and that I would remain awake and alert in all of our travels from that time forth, which I always did! On our subsequent trips, I not only stayed awake, but stood up behind the dash and in front of my mom, all the way to Raymond, much previous to seat belts, of course. As we traveled, I was very cognizant of oncoming cars and had the ability to recognize the make of each automobile as it was still at some distance away. This feat was amazing to the family, and I became quite a celebrity for this skill.

Our vacations to the farm were filled with good times, playing in groves of trees, hiking in the hills, catching frogs and minnows in the coulee streams, riding horses and swimming in the big canal. The large milking barn was a real beauty with a huge hay loft filled with fresh hay, perfect for playing in. We would swing from ropes fastened to the rafters and the steel rail that held the hay slings, and fly into the loose hay. As I have said, my grandfather operated a full-fledged dairy, milking over two dozen cows, and preparing and delivering milk around the town. There were always several hired men to help out and of course to put us boys on calves to ride and help with rounding up cows, and delivering milk. It sure was different than city living, and I loved it.

My grandmother was a good cook, and liked to keep us well fed with lots of goodies and a barrel full of pickles to reach way into through the brine, for a huge dill pickle between meals. She let me help her round up a fat chicken for a Sunday dinner, and then showed me how to remove its head with a sharp axe. I had no qualms about trying it myself. As it was a large family and I being one of the younger ones, it was my luck to sit on an orange crate to eat my meals at the cupboard rather than join the others at the table. I didn't mind that so much, however, the sleeping arrangements were not at all pleasant. I literally ended up "sleeping at the foot of the bed." My uncles took the normal position at the top, and I was required to sleep sideways at their feet with just my head sticking out. This seemed to be the norm back in the good old days. Thank goodness for sleeping bags nowadays.

One of the many trips we made to Raymond was in winter when a few miles past the Town of High River, we ran into a bad snow storm that closed the highway. A number of cars including a Greyhound bus became stranded near a farm home just off the main route, causing the farm people to put everyone up for the night in their warm home. I am not sure how many had a bed to sleep in, but I distinctly remember our family sleeping on the floor huddled up to the kitchen stove for warmth. The snow stopped during the night, and there were quite a number of men digging cars out of the huge drifts. The farmer's wife busied herself, along with others, cooking up a big breakfast while others fed animals and milked the cows. It was a great time for us youngsters. I remember that night with fondness every time we pass that farm, even after these many years.

Brighter Days

THE *HUNGRY THIRTIES* NOW BEING OVER, AND THE *SECOND WORLD War* ended, people were gradually getting back on their feet. Many families lost their precious farms or their hard earned businesses, but most were still strong, and determined to bounce back. However, there were those who were still struggling with heavy debt and losses of family. Life was especially difficult for older folks such as my grandpa who felt he would have to give up the farm. Thankfully my father was now in a position where he could help when his mother and father requested of him to move back to Raymond and buy the dairy and their farm from them and payoff their accumulated debts.

Goodbye to Edmonton, goodbye to city life, we were on our way to a new life with brand-new adventures coming up. With many summers spent on the farm in the past, I was excited for the move. Although I did miss our old haunting grounds, the big ravine, many friends, the busyness of the streets and playgrounds, yet I remember being very happy for the move. It was in the spring of the year, and the school year was well under way, thus being a bit more difficult to orient ourselves into making new friends and getting accustomed to new ways.

To relate another story, being more embarrassing than happy, my first day in my new Raymond school, I was barraged by several of the bigger, older boys. The question was, "what is your name kid?" Simple enough, but being a bit timid in new surroundings, I did not answer immediately. Another tough looking fellow said, "What the hell is your name, kid?" My well-ingrained, nice boy answer was, "I don't speak to boys that swear." Once again I really blew it, having a hard time living it down, until I made a decision. You want tough! You want swear! I'll show you what a big city kid is capable of! Again, the fight was on. I found myself fitting in to the new community and new school, having gained many new friends with this tough kid tactic.

Living on the outskirts of town on a dairy farm brought on a whole new adventure for many of the in town kids. They loved to come out on Saturdays and holidays to play in the trees or roam the coulee and hills. We had lots of adventures and excitement playing on the farm until my dad decided that I was certainly big enough to do some chores and work along with my play. Well I must admit, it was with great mixed emotions for me. My brother Cal was already pulling his weight doing chores, and at age ten, I was expected to join in with him. There were pigs, chickens and calves to feed, horses and milk cows to tend, hay to be cut and hauled to the barn, and before and after school, bottled milk to deliver around town. Woe was me! I thought all of those things were fun when we spent our summer holidays on the farm. However, since my dad now owned the place, the entire family were a part of it and we were expected to do our share of the work. It was but a short time, when I began to realize that all work was not work at all, but much of it was still rather fun. We still filled the hay loft with fresh smelling hay, and I quite enjoyed the process of loading the hayrack with the newly cut hay into large slings, and then sit on top of the load while the rack was pulled into the barn by a team of horses. Subsequently the slings were attached to a hook at the end of the barn and lifted into the loft to be dumped for storage.

At my age, besides helping with hay and other miscellaneous chores, I had the duty of filling the wood box for winter. This was the kindling to start the furnace and kitchen stove fires before coal was placed in the fire box. It seemed to be a never ending task even though we had nearly a forest of trees to gather from. It was probably my least enjoyable job.

I loved working with horses, riding, rounding up cattle to drive to the farm five miles from town, as well as hooking the horses up to a cart, a wagon or a sleigh. Our first years of delivering milk to the public was done with a small milk cart usually pulled by a single horse. I liked winter best of all as we delivered milk around town with a team of two horses hooked on to a bobsled. Our winters were mostly snow or ice covered streets, and made it fun jingling down the road, slipping and sliding around corners. We had to cover the milk bottles with heavy blankets to prevent freezing and the cream at the top popping out of the containers. We especially enjoyed evenings after dark, taking the horses and sleigh out for rides around town, the bobsled loaded with friends or other kids that joined us for the thrill. My dad had a hired man, Cliff Williams, who loved to take turns driving us. He was a good horseman, and really loved to take the corners fast, at times flipping the sleigh box off the runners, giving an extra thrill. Our lives certainly did not consist of all work with no play or adventure time.

We still used horses for much of the work around the farm as well as driving them back and forth between the dairy and the south section located five miles from town. Oft times we herded the dry cows to the pasture awaiting them, with the lush green grass and plenty of water. After calving and freshening them for milking, we trailed the cows back to town. This was one of the more enjoyable things to take care of. There were usually two or three kids from town that liked to join us for the trail ride that took most of the day. Many calves were born each season, thus necessitating branding, tagging and vaccinating each of them. This was always considered to be the big event of the year. The ladies provided a good lunch, while the men and boys wrestled the calves. Some had grown pretty big by the time we got to them, and put up a good fight twisting and kicking. I generally ended the day with a lot of scrapes and bruises. With calves, it wasn't too feasible to use a large squeeze chute, so the deed was taken care of by roping them one by one, throwing them to the ground with generally two of us holding them down, one person branding, while a fourth person did the vaccinating and tagging. It took good team work to get them all taken care of in about two or three days' time. On other occasions we were invited to take part at a larger ranch where beef cattle were raised, to join in on the branding festivities. This was always considered more of a sporting event than a time of work. At times such as this, I became well acquainted with a number of cowboys who loved to participate in the annual rodeos, riding, roping and steer decorating. Having ridden a few calves myself by this time, I decided to try my hand at something a little bigger such as a few old milk cows which really knew how to buck, one jumping in the middle of my stomach almost killing me. They were mean! I later saddled up a few horses that hadn't yet been ridden. They were also mean and knew how to buck, but were a much smoother ride, and eventually settled down. Riding horses became a great passion for me throughout my teenage years, as well as hitching up some of the old work horses to do a job.

As much as I enjoyed riding a saddle horse, or driving a team hauling hay on the dairy farm or around town delivering milk or pulling a bobsled in winter, when it came to traveling to the south farm in a hayrack or wagon, it was a bit much. It was getting time to invest in a tractor, which my father did. He purchased a brand-new John Deere D. It even had rubber tires! Wow, was it ever a beauty. Although we still used the team to cut and rake hay and several other chores, the tractor was much nicer for the harvest. I soon learned how to drive it, as did my brother Cal. We took turns working with it. To start it, one had to turn the huge flywheel on the side to crank it up, not such an easy task. It seemed to be half as big as me. With a lot of effort, I could do it, and then sprint to the seat to take off on this powerful green machine. It moved ahead by the means of a long hand clutch and a set of iron gears. The seat was also metal, but didn't matter much because I had to stand to steer and to reach the clutch. One of my first driving jobs was pulling the grain binder and being warned to be very careful of the power takeoff when I dismounted. I had an uncle who had lost a leg some years before by tangling with such as this. The John Deere diesel proved to be a mighty machine and became very popular with farmers around the country. We were right in style. How proud was I when I putted from the farm into town pulling not one, but two grain tanks behind this powerful machine. Though I had to travel in second gear because the grain tanks were still equipped with iron clad rims and wooden spokes, yet I still felt I was a *King!!*

One of the big issues of living on the outskirts of town was the long walk to school twice a day. We were not allowed to take lunches for noon, so our time to get back and forth was very limited in the hour that we had. We were approximately one and a half miles from school, a long walk for short legs. I was average in size at that time, but it was still a long walk, and what we really needed was a bike. That was one of the next requests of my older sister Dorine, brother Cal and me.

It seemed a simple solution to the problem as we were not allowed to ride horses to school where they would have to be tethered all day. Well our dad was a reasonable man, at times, therefore the request for a bike by Dorine, Cal and me, was being considered. As the coming of Christmas was near at hand, we did have some expectations. My parents, along with best friends, Scott and Ruth Salmon, nearly always made a trip to Great Falls, Montana, to do some Christmas shopping, so this could be it.

Guess what? Sure enough on Christmas morning, there it was. A beautiful shining red Hiawatha bicycle, trimmed in gold, complete with fat tires and long handle bars. Wait! There was only one, addressed to the three of us older siblings. We were so excited, it didn't seem to matter at that moment, but when spring arrived and the weather was more conducive to cycling, the fight was on. Whose turn was it to ride the bike to school, or anywhere for that matter?

While walking home one day, I saw fresh bicycle tracks in the dirt, leading to our house, and day dreamed that the tracks were made by my very own bike. On another occasion when I had anticipated using the bike, my sister Dorine beat me to it, leaving me stranded. I remember taking off on a dead run for two blocks before catching up to her, and then the fight was on as to who should have this glorious machine. Sadly, she won. My dad could see that this was not working out, and consented to the purchase of two older bikes that a neighbor had for sale. Not the best of solutions considering how nice the newer bike was by comparison, but somehow we managed. I liked my horse best anyway.

Cal and I were finally at the age of delivering the milk ourselves, and had an old white Model A Ford panel truck for summer, and of course still used the bobsleigh for winter.

My brother, being two years older than me, thought he should do all of the driving, and that I should do the running into the houses with the milk. Not always fun and certainly not fair. When I complained, it was always "I'll tell dad that you hit me or disturbed me while I was driving." Once in a while he let me drive.

When I was twelve, the local policeman said, "As long as you are driving, you should have a driver's license." He accompanied me to the local license issuing place and for one dollar and no questions asked, told them to issue me a license to drive. The war was just ending and there was a shortage of men to hire for such work.

As time went on, the dairy business increased in volume and it became necessary to turn it into a viable enterprise, complete with a new milk plant building being constructed along with modern day pasteurizing and bottling equipment and a large walk-in cooler and quick-freeze. This not only gave our family more work to do, but also necessitated the hiring of additional hired men. A young Japanese man Tad Watte, and his family were hired to run the milk plant, and an older Dutch family to help us milk the forty plus cows. We finally acquired milking machines, but the cows all had to have a final stripping as well as moving the machines from cow to cow: still lots of work. My father did all of the bookwork and the public relations for the business, and found a bit of time for politics. He was a very hard worker, and expected no less from his sons.

Other than missing out on playing high school basketball or going on all the Boy Scout camps, I felt that I had a pretty full and happy life.

Scouts and Scars

CHURCH ACTIVITIES WERE STILL A VERY IMPORTANT PART OF OUR lives, and none of our family ever missed attending the meetings or being involved in any of the numerous other functions available.

In 1947, the Latter-day Saint Church had a huge Centennial celebration in Salt Lake City, Utah, that involved all, or anyone that could possibly join in to acknowledge the Saints arriving in the Salt Lake Valley. As Boy Scouts, Cal and I had the opportunity to travel with many other Scouts in the back of two grain trucks covered with a wooden canopy and screened in sides. This was an exciting trip that we will always remember, especially the cold sleeping arrangements when we camped.

The main reason sleeping was so cold and uncomfortable on this trip was our sleeping gear. When Cal and I learned that we could join in on this exciting jaunt, we found that sleeping bags were required. Something that every kid has in these modern times but was a rarity in 1947. However, not to be stopped, we obtained an Army Surplus catalogue, wherein they showed all kinds of good stuff. The main thing that caught our eye was surplus sleeping bags, made from a khaki wool and of course used by soldiers in battle. That had to be perfect for our trip, and just $7.00 each. We ordered two of them immediately and were now all set to go. It only took one night to discover that these were only itchy linings, and were not only too thin to be used on hard ground, but had no warmth to them. We found other scouts that were also taken in on this scam. Two nights later we landed on what appeared to be a desert, hot and dry with the only water being large canvas bags hanging here and there in the sun, filled with stale warm almost undrinkable water. We were housed in tents that were scorching hot in the day and freezing cold at night. It was a test of endurance, but after all, we were Boy Scouts, not poor suffering pioneers. The ride back to Canada seemed even longer, not having the same excitement to look forward to.

In summer, we always took time to cool off in the irrigation canal that ran through our pasture. To cross the large coulee that formed part of the pasture was a long flume that carried the water from one side to the other. This made for an additional challenge. We could either bounce along through the water, or when we got brave enough, we would run across the top of the flume, jumping from one cross member to the next, nearly one hundred of them about three feet apart. It was a bit dangerous because of the height of the structure, but a challenge and a lot of fun. Along-side of the new flume, as we called it, there was a very old broken down flume used as a spill way into a pond that fed the coulee stream which we also played in. Being years old, it was lined with thick moss, making it a great slippery slide to zip down into the pond below. One day as I was making a fun trip down, a friend going faster than myself, bumped his feet into my back, thus raising my legs in the air, striking the old wooden side. I received a huge rotted wood sliver into my right leg, about the size of a pencil. Of course it bled profusely and deep enough that it would not be pulled out. Consequently I returned home where my sister tried to get it out and couldn't. She put some iodine on it and a bandage. I didn't want to tell my mom, because it happened on a Sunday, the day we weren't allowed to go swimming. Days later it became badly infected with blood poisoning starting to rise in my leg, I had to tell. I was immediately put in hospital to save my leg by having penicillin pumped into me night and day. After the swelling went down a bit, they operated on my leg, removing the remainder of this near post. Of course my leg was saved and I still carry a large scar as a reminder.

Many interesting adventures took place while growing up on the dairy farm, some fun, many work related, however, as my five years living in Edmonton, life was somewhat of a young boy's paradise. My mom made our home a pleasant place to live. It was always cleaned to perfection and a welcome place to bring friends for a Sunday dinner or just hang out. It was large and well-constructed. We had four bedrooms and an office, roomy kitchen, formal dining room and living room. We also had a four-piece bathroom, but no hot water for the tub. The water was heated on the coal stove and subsequently poured into the bathroom tub, or for the younger kids, into a large tin washtub. We also had a full basement with a huge coal room that held sufficient fuel for the winter. Occasionally the basement was occupied by a family of hired hands, having an outside entry. We were also blessed with an outside biffy at the end of a long path, to be used when the septic tank was full or not working. Our first water was pumped into the house by means of a hand pump. The original lighting was coal oil lamps, but not for too long.

The Arizona Kid and Other Adventures

SCHOOL WAS GETTING TO BE SOMEWHAT DISTASTEFUL TO ME BY THE time I became fifteen years of age, and anyway, I was going to be a farmer/rancher and didn't need all that "book larnin'." At least that was my attitude at the time. As most fifteen year olds, I was also getting to be a handful for my parents to cope with. I skipped school a lot and used work as an excuse when questioned by the school principal. It was on one of these winter days that my buddy Gary Salmon and I decided to drive to our farm for a little fun. The roads were very heavy with snow and many areas of high snowdrifts. I was driving when we came to a large drift; there were tracks through it, but rounded and slick from earlier traffic. I hit the spot going fast, swerving back and forth through the snow when I flipped out of the track at the end of the drift, landing grill first in the deep borrow pit (ditch). The truck came to a sudden stop and careened forward onto its top. That was kind of exciting, until we realized the whole situation and the deep trouble I was in. The truck was less than one year old and was now being used for our milk delivery truck. Wow, it even left the imprint of the grill in the snow. How cool was that? Not cool, but a rather icy response when dad heard about it. We drove out with the three ton truck, up righting it. Luckily because of the heavy soft snow, there was not huge amounts of damage, and it would still run okay. As remarkably predicted, I was in very big trouble; skipping school, taking the truck without permission, rolling the truck over causing a lot of damage to an almost new truck, having to use an older vehicle to deliver milk 'til this one was repaired, and not having enough of my own money to pay for it. That seemed to give some sort of reason for my dad's anger. Now for the *rest of the story!!*

Gary's dad went along with the punishment, which was to prohibit us from using a vehicle for anything but work. No going out evenings for an unspecified time, which to us meant no dating, movies or ball games. Life was ended as we knew it, and there was no way either of us could endure such severe cruelty. We had a plan! We were not that enchanted with the cold winters of Canada and felt that Arizona would be a much more desirable place to live. Besides, we would no longer be under the tyrant ways of our fathers. Our plan was now taking shape. We rode our saddle horses the fifteen miles south of town to the Knight Ranch, where we knew several of the cowboys. We then stabled them in the large horse barn to be looked after until we found the right time to follow up with the rest of our plan. We even lucked out in catching a ride back to Raymond.

Very clever so far. We then rounded up the gear that we knew we would need, consisting of some warm clothes while still in Canada, blankets, new western shirts and jeans, bread and canned food, ropes and rifles and of course a portable radio for tracking our parents news of their hunt for us. The overall idea was that we would saddle up and head across the hills where we could skip the border crossing into the United States. We would then stop at the first ranch that we came to, work there for a few weeks and then move on to the next ranch and do the same, and the next, all the way to our destination of warm inviting Arizona.

For our complete get-a-way, we needed a ride back to the ranch. I borrowed my brother-in-law's pick-up truck for the evening to meet with our girlfriends for a last goodbye and instructions of how we would communicate with them. I had also talked another friend into meeting with us later that night, when we would load our gear into the truck and he could drive us to our immediate destination, the Ranch.

This worked well except for a couple of things. Gary and I saddled up and began our trek across the frozen tundra. Unfortunately for us, the weather temperature dropped to less than thirty degrees along with a cold wind chill. After just a few miles, we knew that we had to turn back and await a warmer day.

We returned to the barn, unsaddled, and stored our precious gear to do some further planning.

Still dark, we saw through a window, headlights from a car, heading toward the horse barn.

It was the car belonging to Gary's dad. We knew this because it was equipped with a spotlight that was zipping around the yard and then back to the barn. How did they know where we were? As it so happened, it began to snow before my friend arrived home from the ranch, driving the truck in the snow, directly to my brother-in-law's house.

About three in the morning, Scott Salmon called to our home to ask if Keith was home. My father said "Of course! He is asleep." Scott then said "You had better check because Gary is not home." When Scott arrived at our house, my dad told him that I had used Floyd's truck that evening, and to see if it was home. It was, with perfect tracks in the snow leading directly to the ranch.

In the meantime, our dads had entered the dark barn and were strolling down the long center aisle toward us. We were determined not to return home with them so each of us picked up a loose 2X4 and standing in a stall on both sides, were about to knock them out and take the car for who knows where? How fortunate that we both decided better and did not go through with it, or we may have killed them or at least caused some serious injury.

The trip home was very silent except for Gary and I whispering our next option. When we arrived home, my father and I were dropped off to finish the incident. I was ready for the worst and stood in the kitchen with fists doubled and awaiting a beating that I was not going to lose. My father however, was very wise, and calmly said, "Let's talk this over."

Well the grounding was lifted, the sanctions lifted, and we started over on a more friendly and liberal basis than had been for some time. The kids at school called me the "Arizona Kid", and Gary, "Rambling Pete."

Life settled down to our usual way of life, and I felt quite content, and was being treated much more as an adult. Even my brother and I were getting along for the most part. The dairy was running smoothly, the farm and the cattle were in good shape, and I was able to take some of our machinery to go out after our harvest and do custom work for other farmers. I earned pretty good money doing this, and enjoyed the chance to work elsewhere than on our home place. I became darn good at handling the big "farm-hand" machine as well as combining and threshing. I loved harvest time anywhere, working both early and late.

One day in the fall, my dad said that he was going to purchase both a new car and a new pickup truck, and that he was going to take delivery of them in Ontario. How would I like to travel with him to drive the truck home? Would I ever! I had never been to Eastern Canada, and that would be such a treat. There was a car transport business in town, and we could ride with a couple of the truckers going back East on one of their trips, and then take delivery of our own vehicles to drive them on home. That served to be a great experience in of itself, and I even got to drive a big rig transport for a goodly number of miles.

Dad had served a Church Mission in Hamilton, Ontario in about 1923, before he was married, and wanted me to see the area, meet some of his acquaintances from that time. But I thought later, that more than anything, he felt it would be a good opportunity for he and I to do something together, and get better acquainted ourselves. What a wonderful idea that was.

We spent several days in Ontario, seeing many interesting things, like the Schwepps Gingerale Plant, the home of the lady that invented the Zipper, the Bell Telephone building and many, many other historic sites. Dad also wanted to take me to a live theater production, but in my stupid youthfulness, I thought a movie theater would be more fun.

All in all, it was a great trip, and seeing a car manufacturing facility was the most interesting of anything else. I am so very appreciative of my father for this wonderful trip, and have wished many times since, that I would have shown more thoughtfulness at the time.

It snowed and we had to drive on many icy highways coming home, but we made it back safely.

By this time I was becoming much more responsible and began to date on a regular basis. I don't remember whom I first dated, but only that I chased around with many different girls, including the one that I was dating at the time of our escapade to go to Arizona. Of course I ultimately went with the most beautiful girl in town, Janice West. She was tall with a great figure, long dark hair and bright blue eyes. She was two years younger than me, but belonged to a large family of older brothers that took very good care of her. I might say, that I also did. We were quite inseparable, and not only hung out at school, but ball games, movies and church functions. She was a mathematics genius and I was exceptionally good in English. Between the two of us, we did our homework together in record time. We also spent a lot of time either at her home or mine. She loved the farm as much as I did and helped with the haying and picking rock from the fields. We went together as a steady couple for better than two years, and always felt that we would marry someday. Her brother, Alan, just older than me, and I, also became very good friends and still are to this day.

We eventually parted company for reasons that I don't remember, but I did start dating a girl from the town of Magrath (our rival town). At the time, the Raymond boys were dating Magrath girls and Magrath guys were dating Raymond girls. None of us seemed to like the idea, but that was what was happening. It gave us an excuse to fight with someone. I distinctly remember one time of chasing some Magrath boys home. While driving side by side, I told Gary to take the wheel while I leaned way out, punching a Magrath kid in the face a couple of times. We were driving about 60 miles an hour at the time on the gravel

Don't try this today ~~highway~~. ~~Another stupid trick, was jumping from one pickup truck to another going~~ the same direction, also at a speed of about fifty to sixty ~~miles per hour. Why were we still alive?~~ ?

About the time that I completed high school, I thought that I should take a welding course at SAIT, in Calgary, and more than anything, get me away from Raymond for a while. Along with my friend, Ed Kubota, we enrolled for a three-month course. We rented a one-room apartment from an elderly couple who lived across the street from the school, making it handy for us, as we didn't have a vehicle for transportation. We were also scrimping on funds and were confined pretty close to the area with only an occasional bus trip downtown. This was very difficult for a couple of teens who had vehicles for the last couple of years in which to come and go as we wanted. Worse yet, we barely scraped by on money for food. It all served to be a good learning experience for us. Being hungry and resourceful, we walked down to the corner restaurant where we would order a bowl of soup with all of the crackers we could eat, filled our soup with free crackers and catsup and ate 'til we were satisfied.

Another source of food came with a further spark of inspiration. We attended our Sunday church meetings hoping for some kind souls to take pity on us and invite us for a family dinner. This worked well, and we stuffed ourselves with all of the good food we could hold, hoping it would last a few days. It didn't quite last that long, but at least we could tell our parents that we were attending church. Sacrificing many of the things that I had enjoyed made me appreciate life much more. I determined to work hard and make this time count for something worthwhile. I passed the course with a ninety percent mark as did my friend Eddie. My welding ability proved to be worthwhile on the farm when I returned home.

When my brother Cal turned nineteen, he was called on a two-year Church Mission to New Zealand. He was really excited for the call, particularly because our Uncle Lorin had served there sometime during the twenties. I was also excited because Cal would be out of my hair for a couple of years. For the most part, Cal and I had been good pals, but he always seemed to have the edge on any conflict.

It did however put a heavier workload on me but I felt equal to it. I worked farmland, planted grain, and did a lot of the harvesting. By this time, Dad seemed to have enough hired hands around to handle the dairy end of things, milking cows, processing the milk in the plant, and most of the milk delivery. I, in turn, still enjoyed putting up hay along with the fieldwork.

By this time my dad had become quite involved in a small insurance business on the side that was occupying a lot of his time. He then began to entertain the idea of selling the dairy portion of the operation, and just keep the farm. The insurance business was also growing so he knew that would keep him plenty busy enough. Besides that, he loved being politically active which also occupied a lot of time. One of the hired families were interested in buying the dairy, Cliff Williams and two of his brothers, so the negotiations were started. I am sure that if either Cal or myself had been older, perhaps married or working on our own, that one or both of us would have wanted to buy the dairy for ourselves. It was 35 acres in a prime location and in this day would have been extremely valuable, even as an acreage. An established dairy business fully modernized meant further value. My dad however, was anxious to be out of the business, and wanted to move on with other pursuits. It took nearly a year for everything to get put together for a final sale, and I, in the meantime, continued to work the farm.

Fond Memories

FUNERAL FOR CLIFF (handwritten)

To Elsie Williams and Family:

Cliff "Grump" Williams, my second dad. My memories of you, Cliff, are so many and so varied that I could almost fill a book. My memories of Cliff and Elsie go back to the late forties and early fifties and then on up to the present. The most in depth time being that time spent on my father's dairy and on the farm and on top of the Ridge. I was a teenager with all of the vim and vigor of youth, growing and developing and not wanting always to listen to my own father, but needing a swift boot in the rear-end by someone – and Cliff, that "someone" was you. You taught me to ride a horse, taught me to milk a cow, to brand, to dehorn, to put up hay, to wrestle and ride calves – I was never great at roping, but I could catch a calf if I had to. You even taught me to say shit if it was necessary and if I managed to have a mouth full of it from wrestling with the cattle. You also taught me later on to be a good home teacher.

My very fondest memories are cattle drives to the Milk River Ridge or to the farm on a warm sunny day and returning to our horses in the cool quiet of the evening when we would discuss everything from cows and horses and putting up hay, to girls and how I should treat them. I also have fond memories of fixing fence together and of the hundreds of hours in the hay field, and hauling hay to the dairy barn with our hayracks and teams of horses and pulling the hay into the loft with slings, and tripping the slings before on occasion, burying one of us in the hay. I remember some of your cowboy buddies, Mote, Cactus, and Dooly helping us with the hay and milking cows, and then roping the calves afterwards.

In later years as your High Priest Group Leader, I enjoyed your friendship and your loyalty as you did your home teaching and fulfilled your duties and assignments in our quorum.

You were a dear friend and a great listener and teacher when as a youth I needed additional fatherly advice when I was too timid to go to my own dad, or he was busy with other situations. Later on in my life, even my own sons enjoyed the horseback scout trips with you as they grew up, and talk about those times with fondness.

Thanks Cliff for being you – we'll ride together again someday.

Just one more friend,
Keith L. Hancock

A Work and a Mission

It was the fall of 1951, and we had a beautiful grain crop when winter weather came roaring in. Fortunately, we had our grain cut in stooks awaiting further ripening to be threshed. The cold blizzard conditions didn't let up for the remainder of winter, and we found ourselves along with almost all other farmers, awaiting spring, to complete our harvest. In the month of February of 1952 we had a bit of a break in the weather, and set up our threshing machine, tractors and wagons for a cold harvest. There was still a lot of snow in the field and piled up on the grain stooks, but it had warmed up a bit, so we went to work. I of course was the farm-hand operator, and the other men handled the unloading of the racks, and kept the big threshing machine operating, with two others hauling the grain. I normally enjoyed running the farmhand (a large loading unit attached on to a tractor) with its eight-foot tines. However, as I ran about the snowy field picking up the bundles, the cold wet snow would fly in my face, getting me soaking wet. We finally got the job done with a pretty good return, even though I ended up with pneumonia. Older people to this day still talk about the blizzard and harvest of 1951.

Later that summer, I turned 19 years old, the age of being called to a Church mission. I was then back to dating Janice, thinking that I was old enough to get married, and forget a mission. But then Janice was just seventeen, and a bit young for marriage. Two more years would make this prospect just right.

I dutifully put my papers in for serving a mission, but was still not completely convinced that this was what I wanted to do. I went through the usual series of interviews to check my worthiness, and was sure that I would not pass the tests. However, the Lord had other plans for me, and all of the authorities said yes. The real clincher came when Apostle Spencer W. Kimball happened to be in our community for a stake conference, and took the opportunity to personally interview all of the prospective missionaries. That was tough. He even pounded the desk with his fist when he said, "Are you sure you are not lying to me?" At that moment, I thought he was the meanest man on earth, but later learned to love and respect him, knowing that he was a servant of God.

About the middle of August, my call arrived and I was still a little sceptical about accepting a call. I had made up my mind that if I was called to an area close to home, I would not go. I gingerly opened the envelope. My eyes caught the word *Argentina*, how could I possibly turn down an opportunity to travel half way around the world and learn another language? Best of all it was warm.

My brother Cal was not yet home from New Zealand, and I thought I should wait for him to get back. However, my folks were so happy to get me away from trouble and on a mission they said I should leave my truck, my horse and my sweetheart, and GO.

My call was to be in Salt Lake City the first part of September, just when we would be starting harvest and also moving from the dairy to a big beautiful home in town. It was the gorgeous home of Lottie Knight, widow of Raymond Knight. It was the biggest and nicest home in Raymond. I had admired it all of my life, and now how could I miss out on this. It was built for the late Ray Knight, who was a millionaire at the time. It was a one and a half story with a finished basement, making it close to six thousand square feet.

Well, it took a couple of weeks to get everything moved, and my parents were recarpeting the entire new home and buying mostly new furniture and window coverings, so it would be a slow process.

I had a big list of clothes that I had to acquire, along with luggage, and worst, or best, I had to spend a whole lot of time with Janice. I wasn't ready for such a big change, and it would be for two and a half years, not just two as was Cal's mission. Because of learning a new language, the foreign missions were an extra six months. As it turned out, we did get moved to the new house, but I only slept there two nights.

I had only been to Salt Lake twice, and was very much of a novice when it came to travelling out of the country, but being young and adventurous, I was ready to try anything.

There I stood somewhere in the middle of a huge city, dressed in a suit of all things, holding a big suitcase in one hand, and even worse than in a suit, in the other hand, I held a felt dress hat, yuck!

What on earth was this country bumpkin doing? My folks had been busy moving into the new house as well as harvest beginning, so the alternative was for my buddy Gary, along with my sweetie, Janice, to drive me to Great Falls to catch a bus for Salt Lake. What a send-off for a somewhat reluctant missionary. Do I hunt for the Mission Home, or hop on another bus headed for my dream state of Arizona? Well I had come this far alone, so I should at least give it a try. After all, Argentina, South America, still sounded pretty good. Perhaps when I arrived there I could still find a big ranch to work on, and nobody would ever find me. But then there was Janice. I wondered how long it would take for her to come to Argentina. Oh well, I was here now, just two blocks from the Mission Home, so I learned by now. Besides I was hungry and tired. I should get a little rest and do a bit more planning. I walked to the Home, my suitcase was very heavy, and it was good to be greeted by a bunch of other "greenies."

Two days into the routine, I was starting to feel a part of the procedure, and there were several pretty nice guys, in fact two of them from Cardston, a town 35 miles from home.

One evening, one of the fellows said that his parents only lived a few blocks from where we were staying, and that they had a television set. A what! I had only heard of them, but to this point had not actually seen one. He suggested that we walk to his house for an evening of TV, pictures on a box.

Sounded great to me. About six of us joined in for the excitement. The room was darkened, the 12- inch machine turned on, the Indian Chief head faded, and there we were, watching an oblong brownish, yellowish picture. I don't remember what the program was, but I was totally mesmerized with such an electronic age miracle.

After a week of orientation, we all left the warmth and security of a place with great meals and good fun, for the train station; three of us heading for New York City, while others left for a variety of other locations. I had never been on a train before, and now I was on my way to one of the world's largest cities to board a ship to take me to a land I had only dreamed of, in South America. The land of big ranches, lots of cattle and gauchos. Zooming across prairies, lakes and mountains was almost more of a thrill than my days of buzzing Main Street in Raymond on a Saturday night. As we travelled both night and day, we were approached periodically by a military police asking for I.D., and how come we were not in uniform? It was a time during the Korean War, when most guys our age were serving in the military. We were quite frowned upon.

Several great stops and transfers occurred along the way. The first big one was two days in Chicago, where we had time to tour the city in a limo. We drove through a very unsavoury neighbourhood of burned out buildings, old mattresses on the streets with people sleeping on them, while other people just stared at us with blank expressions. Our driver maintained that should we stop for any reason that it would be an end of the car and us. We never tested it out! We also had the privilege of attending a Major League baseball game of the Chicago White Sox.

Our next big stop was near Niagara Falls, where, after taking a bus to see them and back, we had to run to catch the train already on the move, but we did barely make it. Then there was New York City, amazing New York City. Only in the movies did I ever dream of seeing such a place. It was everything I ever dreamed it would be, including the noise of the busy streets. And would those huge buildings ever hold a *lot of hay*. We had a three day lay over before our ship was to sail, and had a lot of time on our hands to experience a few of the sights and sounds of this metropolis. We toured several museums, went to Time Square, and the Rockefeller Center. We also took an elevator to the very top of the Empire State building, and later spent quite a bit of time walking through Central Park. Another thing that fascinated me was walking through the fruit and vegetable stands, and seeing the large trucks unloading their wares. It should have made me homesick, but it didn't! Although I must admit, I did miss Janice and wished she could share all of these sights with me.

After a three day wait, and not having a lot more money, I was ready to embark on the ship. By today's standard, it was small, and certainly not a cruise ship, but for me at that time, it was big. It was called the SS Uruguay.

Three weeks at sea, quite an experience for a prairie farm boy, but I didn't get seasick, nor even close to it. The meals were incredible and all you could eat and then even more. Our table waiter was a short plump Chinese fellow, who said, "You eat 'em, I bring 'em." We did take him up on his offer, and kept him busy hauling trays of food to us. When we would return to our cabin, there were also more snacks, including lots of fresh fruit. There was also a nice pool on board, and I was able to soak up lots of sunshine on my already tanned muscular body. Our first stop was at the island of Trinidad for one day where we could wander the sites of the South Seas. Our next port was the beautiful and amazing Rio de Janeiro. Pulling into port was the most beautiful sight I had ever seen in my life. The water was bluer than anything I could even imagine with the whitest sand ever, bordering the vast ocean. We came into a large bay with Sugarloaf Mountain towering high above. The terrain was peaked with these towering formations fully covered with lush greenery of every description. I should imagine Heaven looking somewhat like this. We took a tram to the top of Sugarloaf to view the ocean and countryside, and to eat a snack at the luxurious restaurant. Another night on the ship, and then another day sightseeing around the city, taking time for a swim in the ocean. A big mistake for me. We went to the famous Copacabana Beach, where I daringly went directly into the warm water. I had never been in an ocean before and waded out to my neck, walking on the smooth soft sand. A wave struck me, filling my lungs with salt water, as I came up gasping for air. Another wave hit me, moving me further out and causing me to swallow even more water. I was not a great swimmer at best, and thought that was the end, when a companion who was an ocean swimmer, came out and pulled me to shore. Needless to say, I now have a great respect for ocean swimming.

We arrived at the Port of Buenos Aries in Argentina October 8th, 1952, where my mission experiences started with the startling revelation that all countries weren't free like ours. When going through the customs entry, my suitcase was roughly opened, and my belongings scattered all about the counter, not having regard for any of my personal property. I was about to lose my temper and spout off to them, when the Elder who met me at the customs, cautioned me not to say anything. That is just what happens here. Being a dictatorship country, this was not Canada nor the United States. After the official took a few of my things for himself, I was left to stand with my mouth open, cram my clothes back in, shut my case and move on. We then left the customs building to a waiting city bus to take us out of the fenced in compound where we got off to be taken to a small booth to be thoroughly searched before hitting the actual street.

This was the city and country where I would spend my next three years (I extended my mission to three years). President Juan Peron, was the Dictator of Argentina. Living and working on a ranch was becoming more appealing to me all the time. After my first half hour in this country, I would serve my mission and go home to my sweetheart and my saddle horse, and even endure the cold weather.

My Mission President was Harold Brown from Utah and was coming within a few months of the end of his term. He had been a former FBI agent, and was a bit stern, however, a good man, with a nice wife. The Mission Home was pleasant with a good atmosphere and several special assisting Elders being temporarily called to help out with the desk type of work.

After spending a short time at headquarters, I was assigned to a senior companion, Elder Robert Worthen of Salt Lake. He was a great guy with an amiable personality, just who I needed to get me started. He was a good teacher, but unfortunately was nearing the end of his mission and would be leaving for home in less than two months. I had never studied a foreign language in school, and was struggling somewhat with speaking Spanish (known as Castilian), and had to rely heavily on the Lord for the help I needed. Neither had I been very studious where the Gospel was concerned, and had to do a lot of praying about that as well. If I was to get through my mission with any kind of success, I needed to forget myself, and get to work. I wasn't used to failing at the things I started, and this wasn't going to be one of them. In learning to speak well, there were always pretty young girls who loved to taunt the new missionaries with their wily words and cute little smiles and laughter. I thought at first that every sentence seemed to be two feet long with no break in between.

After three months, I was transferred to the city of San Nicolas, about 40,000 people, with a new companion, Elder William Wood, 6'7" tall. He was raised in Mexico with perfect Spanish.

Our virtual size difference made it difficult for us to work together, looking odd walking down the street, particularly being foreigners. My only salvation to this was the fact that in Argentina, I was considered average size if not a little taller than most of the native Argentines. We were companions for several months and got along fairly well, even though we had many differences. I was quite happy when we finally received a transfer. The only problem with this transfer was that I remained in the same city, but my new companion was an Argentine Elder who spoke no English whatsoever. His name was Amadeo Cortese, a fine man and much shorter than me, which was fine. My Spanish was tolerable at that time, however, not fluent by any means. He wasn't about to learn English, so I had to improve my skills in his language. If I ever had to lean on the Lord, it was then. I was down on my knees constantly asking for divine help. It slowly came, and we became quite effective missionaries.

One of my first experiences in that vast open range country was a day trip to the real live pampas. I had looked forward to getting out of the city and seeing the ranching country that I had always read about in school and dreamed of being in the thick of it all. Our city of Tandil had been tracted out many times and we, with some encouragement on my part, felt that perhaps it might be more fruitful to hit the land. It was a scorching hot day, but the sky was clear, the grass was tall and green, and best of all, there were cattle and horses grazing on the loose. It was a gorgeous day, and my heart was almost thumping through my shirt. Every now and then we came to a small road leading from the main dirt road, to a little insignificant looking little adobe hut. There was always a few native or gaucho looking people sitting around in the shade, some chickens in the yard, and maybe a skinny looking horse staked out or tied to a rail. Was there any point in visiting these poor people? Well after all, they were also God's children and deserved a chance at hearing our message. That was the reason we walked these miles in the blazing heat. We did stop in at several of these humble little homes, and found a delightful reception at almost all. Although I was still struggling with the language, my companion being from Argentina, had no problem explaining who we were and why we were there. Most could read, and were happy to receive some brochures and a copy of the Book of Mormon with a promise to follow up.

After several hours of walking on the dusty roads, my feet began to swell with blisters on nearly every inch. I had worn some shoes that were fairly new and not broke in. I began to fill them with Articles of Faith cards, handkerchiefs, or grass, anything I could find to stuff in them next to my feet. I took them off to walk barefoot, but between dirt clods and thistles, this did not sooth them. As we came to another farm or estancia, I put my shoes back on and hobbled over to the house. Many hours later, we arrived back at our Branch where I could soak my feet and doctor them up. Other than my ruined feet, we felt quite successful with our day in the pampas of Argentina. All in all, I was elated with this day, and would do it over again. Maybe, just an outside maybe, Heavenly Father might step in and help some of these sweet humble souls grasp the concept of the Gospel, and follow into His great plan that is meant for all of His children.

As a Canadian (only two of us in all of the mission), I was required to fly out of the country every three months to renew my visa. The Americans could remain for one year at a time. I had to stay overnight at the Montevideo Mission Home, and then return the following day, where my passport was then re-stamped and good for another three months. My first trip out after three months was very frightening as my language was still pretty shaky. I had been to the Mission Home once only on the way down, and that was by car, and in a city of over one million people. I thought that I could just catch a city bus and recognize where to exit. Wrong! After riding for about one-and-a-half hours, I decided I missed my stop, got off, couldn't make myself understood, and with a humble frightened prayer, I started to walk in an unfamiliar direction. I walked and walked for more than two hours, with darkness coming on I really became nervous. I was just beginning to revamp my plan, and there it was, looking like the best site I had ever seen. What a welcome I received.

The seaplanes that travelled the half hour trip from Argentina to Uruguay were ancient and should have been in mothballs years before, but still in use. One trip that I took over the years, the windshield popped out, causing us to return. Another trip, an engine caught fire, returning us to base.

As the planes left the water port, they dug down into the sea, shaking and rattling, just ready to call it quits. They all did make it, and here I am.

It was always quite an experience coming back into the country after being away. The same old searching luggage or briefcases, asking scary questions in a language that I was still a bit unfamiliar with. Also the usual frisking when leaving the Customs office. After my many trips back and forth, I was finally getting used to the routine. Luckily my American counterparts only had to do this once per year, and usually were several of them together. While as a Canadian, I had to go it alone.

Before I leave my experiences of travelling to Uruguay, I will relate one that took place a year later. An important thing that we could take care of for our mission while in Montevideo was to exchange our American currency for Argentine pesos. In Argentina, one dollar would trade for fifteen pesos, while on the Uruguay market, one dollar would buy thirty pesos, double the amount. Therefore while on my one-day trip, I would take several hundred dollars with me for exchange. On this particular trip, our Mission Home wished to buy a building to use as a church facility, and handed me twelve thousand dollars to exchange. That amount of cash made me feel somewhat nervous, however, I had no problem in the past, and felt that by now I was pretty cool and could handle the situation. It was not illegal to do this, only that a young person with that much money was apt to simply disappear along with the cash in this dictatorship country. I had the money stashed in shoulder holsters under my jacket, and went through customs without a hitch. I then boarded the awaiting bus to leave the compound, it started to move forward, and I leaned back with a sigh of relief. Just then the shrill sound of a police whistle resounded in my ears, I came up with a start and began perspiring about my collar. What was this about? Two policemen climbed on board and began searching people as they came toward the rear of the bus, just where I was sitting. Two ladies were sitting on the seat just ahead of me, the police checked their purses, ordering them off the bus. Once again my fervent prayers were answered, and my trembling stopped. I never found out what the ladies had, nor what happened to them. I was okay, as was the Mission's money.

To add just a touch more to this intrigue, during the days of Dictator Juan Peron, it was fairly well known that scores of people who were a problem to the Country, just simply disappeared from sight.

We were further made aware of this situation when living in the City of Eva Peron, a city of many government establishments. Our lights periodically dimmed at infrequent intervals or went out completely for several minutes. We were often curious about this, when a government official who had become friends with the missionaries, informed us that the unmarked ominous looking building on our block was actually a place where electrical torture took place. We had often seen police vehicles come and go from there. It wasn't particularly a secret from the general public. As a matter of interest, fifteen years later, we were still hearing the same type of stories of disappearing persons in Argentina. Of course as missionaries, we had no proof of these stories, nor were we looking to prove them.

Interestingly enough, a few months later, while my junior companion, Elder Kent Jolley (who several years after our missions became a General Authority in the Church) and I were tracting in the large city of Lujan, we decided to enter a gated residential area of the city to perhaps recruit a more upper class of investigators. Wrong! We approached the door of the chief of police, who immediately marched us the three blocks down the street to his office and the local jail for questioning and identification. I don't think he was much frightened of us as he didn't recruit any help, however, being in a dictatorship country, we were somewhat nervous. After missionary identification, lots of explanations and about two-and-a-half hours later, we were free to go, but not to his personal area. We didn't gain a convert out of him, but who knows, maybe later he became curious.

One of the reasons we decided to tract this particular city, was because of the Catholic cathedral. It is claimed to be the largest of its kind in South America, and to date had never had our LDS missionaries stationed there. The cathedral was monstrous and the architecture was phenomenal. Inside of this huge building the walls were adorned with crutches, canes, wheel chairs, airplane propellers and every kind of handicapped prop you can think of. These were to signify healings and rescues of people. While outside, along with dozens of tourist selling kiosks, selling statues, candles, rosaries, crosses, etc., were sidewalks inundated with people, most crawling, or hobbling one or two blocks to the marble stairs entering the cathedral, stopping to pray every few yards. Some of the folks had bleeding knees and hands from the arduous ordeal. They obviously had more faith in being healed than I, but obviously worked for some.

One of the situations that had taken place in this otherwise beautiful country was the death of Evita Peron, former wife of President Juan Domingo Peron. She had risen from one of the dregs of society, to a powerful position as the dictator's wife. She was beautiful, talented, and extremely smart. Unfortunately she contracted cancer during her fame, and passed away quite suddenly, leaving the whole country in a state of mourning. It was the custom, and became law to stand in silence for two minutes in her memory, at the start of any and all public functions. Evita was regarded as a Saint, not only to the President, but to most of the countrymen. Huge posters of her adorned the streets, public buildings and all transportation facilities.

In February of 1954, we had a very special visitor to our Mission Field, that of our beloved President and Prophet, David O. McKay. As I had been called to be a Branch President, I had the privilege of meeting with him personally for an interview and private visit, a very nice experience for me.

Argentina, being under strict rule of a dictatorship, would not allow public meetings of more than 12 people in a single gathering without first obtaining a permit. This applied to private parties, schools, weddings, or Church meetings, whatever the occasion. While President McKay was visiting, our church of course wished to hold a state-wide conference. Getting permission to do so was not as much of a problem as it was to locate a building large enough to hold the several thousand people that were expected. President Valentine, along with President McKay, decided to go right to the top, and obtained an audience with President Peron, a difficult feat in of itself. However, being the leader of a prominent church, the meeting was granted. Peron said to them, "I know that you do not drink alcohol, tea or coffee, so what can I serve you?" President McKay told us later that he had been in the presence of kings, presidents and rulers of many countries, but had never been treated more graciously than by President Peron. During the meeting, President Peron asked "What can I do for you? Anything special that you would like, I will make available to you!"

After explaining the plight of not having a large building to meet in, President McKay was told that the Colon Theatre could be made available for our use. This theatre is the largest and finest in South America, and is booked sometimes two years in advance. All previous performances were then cancelled for two days, and the theatre was turned over for our sole use. The huge building contained plush velvet seats, carpets and draperies, individual box seating balconies, and all of the fineries that could be built into such a structure.

Thousands of people attended the two days of meetings, many were curiosity seekers to see and hear a Prophet of God. There were also many plainclothes policemen in the audience to report on the procedures of the meetings. President McKay spoke for two hours in each of the meetings keeping us all spellbound. His son, Robert, translated for him in the first session, with President Lee Valentine interpreting the second. If I ever had any doubts before about the veracity of the Church, they were all laid to rest after this very special spiritual experience. The following day, our one hundred or so missionaries attended a testimony meeting that lasted ten hours with only a short lunch break.

As the months rolled on, we were visited by other General Authorities, all having wonderful messages and spiritual advice for us. I also became much more effective as a missionary in the next year or so. The Korean War being over, many more missionaries were sent to our Mission, and it meant that as one of the older ones, I would have two or three junior companions at one time instead of the usual one. This seemed to work quite well, and I enjoyed trying to teach them and look out for their needs. In one of my several Branches, we were assigned to locate two families that were on the "less active" list. As it turned out, they both lived on farms well out of the city. My then companion and I both had bicycles and thought it to be a challenge to ride into the campos looking for them. As we travelled, we found ourselves in almost desert like terrain with nothing more than sand and cactuses. Houses were very far away from each other and were not much more than little two room mud and straw huts with maybe a tree or two for shade from the unforgiving hot sun. I found it most interesting to see a shallow trench around the whole perimeter of the house, and in my questioning, I discovered that the custom was to lean a chair against the side of the house to sit in the shade, and follow around the house just ahead of the sun as it moved forth.

We didn't have much luck finding our members, but enjoyed the experience. On our way home we came upon a couple of ostriches running across the sand and decided to chase after them on our bikes. Not a chance, I think they can outrun a horse, and decided that is why the Gauchos use boladores to throw at their legs, wrapping them into a ball. I haven't actually seen it done, but I understand they are very expert at the catch.

We worked hard at our missionary duties, but also took a little time to sight see and take pictures. One of my delightful trips was to drive to a huge ranch with a well to do rancher, going from villa to villa while still on his vast property. Each villa was occupied by gauchos and their families that had a certain area and number of cattle to care for. We stopped in the afternoon for an asado (barbeque) of beautiful Argentine beef, and cooked to perfection on a unique homemade grill.

I was ecstatic to drive across the plains viewing thousands of head of well fed cattle, and then climb on the back of a horse to take a short break from a bicycle and soft living. It was a moment that I had always dreamed of in my youth, but never in my wildest imagination ever thought it would come about, not even for an hour or so. Gaucho saddles are made with a wood base, covered with a broad sheep skin tied down with leather. Soft, but almost uncomfortable stretching your legs over the wide expanse. The bridles are basically a leather halter with no bit. A fantastic experience for this cowboy.

In thinking about my mission, I thought perhaps I really didn't do much good for anyone but myself, however, as I recount some experiences, maybe something may have come from it. I did have the opportunity to baptize eight persons in total, not that many, but if they all stuck with the Church, and possibly bring some family or friends in, it will have been great. One convert baptism in particular was a man and his wife by the name of Jose de San Martin, a direct descendant of General Jose de San Martin, the liberator of Argentina in the mid 1800s. These were older people, but very enthused about the church as well as his relationship to the original San Martin, of which he had traced back.

One never knows what may come of this relationship in future times.

I had been scheduled for release from my South American Mission in two-and-a-half years from my start date. However, the mission was in short supply of senior missionaries, and a good friend of mine, Colin Miller from Taber, Alberta had arrived six months after me, and it was our wish to travel home together by way of a trip to Europe. The request had to be okayed by the authorities from Salt Lake, and fortunately they gave permission. It simply meant that I would have to remain an extra six months. Probably my best six months in so far as my dedication to missionary work was concerned. When our day of release came, President Valentine arrived at the ship dock to see us off and to extend to us our official release certificates. At that time, a missionary was released right in the mission field, where as now, it is done when you arrive home.

Continental Cuisine and More

OUR TRIP BEGAN WITH A TWENTY DAY CRUISE ABOARD A MUCH smaller ship than we had arrived on, but was fun and lots of great food as our previous ship. It had a pool, a nice deck and lounge. We had few stops, one at the Canary Islands where we disembarked for a day, and just two or three others stops before we came to our final destination, disembarking in Hamburg Germany. Sadly in 1955, there were still many scars and signs of World War II, not only in the harbors displaying the remains of destroyed and half sunken ships, and other debris throughout the entire city. It was still strung with heavy barbed-wire and fenced in barricades everywhere, but worse yet, bombed out commercial buildings, cathedrals and houses. The war was a horrible thing to contemplate and see the actual left over signs. It made me heart sick viewing these pathetic ruins.

To get by as inexpensively as we could, we looked for Bed and Breakfast places, and found them to be plentiful and reasonable. They were not fancy, some even equipped with straw ticks for mattresses.

I had slept on a lot worse. We found great food in the cafes cheap and filling, with huge portions.

Our next step was to rent a car and begin our travels. We had no trouble finding a rental garage, but a language barrier presented a bit of a problem. However, we convinced the man that although we were young, we were very dependable. He said that his rentals were all out but that he would pick up a brand new Volkswagen beetle for our use. There were no mileage restrictions attached to our contract, all we had to do was put gas in it and go. Just what we needed for at least a month tour.

After nearly sixty years, I don't remember many details, but we did travel throughout Germany, France, Spain, Belgium, Luxemburg, Austria, Switzerland and Italy. Of course in all of these countries, we stopped at the more renowned cities and places. The Eiffel Tower in Paris, the Vatican and the Sistine Chapel in Rome, the magnificent 17 foot marble statue of the David in Florence, bullfight in Madrid, the Simplon Pass between Switzerland and Italy, marvellous city of Venice in Italy, taking a ride on a gondola, and swimming in the beautiful blue water on the sea coast of the French Riviera. We of course also went into the gigantic Coliseum as well as climbed to the top of the leaning tower of Pisa. Plus more numerous places that we experienced.

We returned the car approximately a month later with many thousands of miles registered on it. The man in his broken English told us that the car was "kaput," and did not want to return our deposit. This did not sit well with me as we needed all of our money to continue our trip. I had a bit of a physical scuffle with him to finally retrieve our deposit. I still had a bit of temper left in me.

After Europe, we travelled to London to spend about another week. I had already made up my mind that I would not like England still because of silly teenage prejudices. I loved it although it was somewhat difficult to understand their heavy accent. I am sure they feel the same way about us Canadians.

We soon discovered another Bed and Breakfast location, but found the breakfast to be pretty slim for a couple of healthy young men. After touring Europe, we found all of the food to be small portions by comparison.

By this time we were both nearly out of money and had to call home for a bit of a refill. After my parents not having seen me for nearly three years, they were anxious for my homecoming and didn't hesitate to get a few bucks to me. Colin's parents were the same.

While in London we saw the many sites available there, including Buckingham Palace, the Tower of London, Big Ben, the Subways, and rode on a Double Decker bus. We also attended the live theatre production of "The King And I," most impressive and dramatic. It was another great city to visit, another monumental experience before returning home to become a couple of small town farm boys.

This trip was by plane, as we flew from London to New York with a short layover at Dublin, Ireland. This added one more country to our growing list, although there was not enough time for a tour of Ireland. From the air, Ireland was beautiful and green, a place I would have liked to extend my visit.

We landed in this notorious huge city of New York in early evening, in plenty of time to check into a hotel. Once again we both called home for a little more financial help, not enough to fly home but sufficient for a long hot bus trip to Alberta.

Before leaving New York, we had two days to wander the streets and once again take in the wonders of a gigantic town. Of course going to the top of the Empire State building was a must along with Coney Island and Central Park. One of the more fascinating places for me to walk around was the large market areas where fresh fruit and vegetables were sold. It never ceased to amaze me as to how and when all of those products arrived for sale so early in the mornings. One night I left our hotel room by myself at about two o'clock in the morning to walk through these market places to see what went on during the night. I found to my delight and curiosity that large farm produce trucks pulled into these dozens of stalls, and unloaded everything from potatoes to watermelons, to chickens, plus flowers and hundreds of other consumable items. I was informed later that it was not wise for me to wander these areas alone in the wee hours. I never gave it a thought at the time, but enjoyed seeing all of this take place. It even made farming look more glamorous to me.

We at last felt that we were ready for the scary trip home to our families. After being away for three years, I was anxious to get home, but at the same time, I felt somewhat nervous about arriving back to my former life. I knew that things would be very different for me, my former girlfriend had married, my brother and brother-in-law had taken over the reins of the farm, my horse had been sold, along with the pick-up truck that I had driven for a couple of years, and my parents had moved into their new home, just as I had left. Wow, did I really want to go back to all of these changes?

Home Again, Home Again

THE RIDE WAS JUST AS WE HAD EXPECTED, ONLY MORE SO. It was extremely hot, with no air conditioning in those years, very long (sleeping on the bus two nights), and very uncomfortable. We first arrived in the town of Taber, where Colin lived. The streets were still gravelled, and the wind was blowing at about 90 km per hour, with nothing to see but dirt and dust. My good friend and travelling companion stood in the midst of this with suitcase in hand, hollered back to me, in jest, but half serious, "I want to get back on the bus and keep going!" Looking out at the sight, I very much felt the same. The next stop of course was Lethbridge, where I would be dropped. Now I was really nervous. The wind was still blowing when I retrieved my suitcase and walked to a phone booth that was rattling and banging so loud, I thought it would blow over with me still inside. I shakily dialled the number of our home, if I remembered it correctly. "Hello Mooomm, this is your son, Keith. I am in Lethbridge at the bus depot." I felt I would collapse! "Oh son, it is so good to have you home. Your dad and Cal are in Lethbridge at a machine dealer shop. Can you find it?"

I wasn't sure I could, but started walking down the street to where, I wasn't certain, when I bumped into an older cousin. After exchanging greetings, I asked him where the shop was where I could meet my dad and my brother whom I had not seen in five years. He said he knew and to hop in his car and he would take me there.

49

It was strange but an exciting and affectionate meeting after so many years being away, and so many changes in all of our lives, mostly for much better.

The ride home was comfortable and chatty in my dad's new Oldsmobile 98, and my brother, now much heavier and bigger than me, and now a married man with one young son. How would I ever catch up and be his equal since he had now taken over the running of the farm? My dream of becoming a farmer and rancher may never happen. My father had also now expanded his insurance business, complete with a new office and lots of clientele, and he sure would like me to enter the insurance business with him. I wasn't even home yet before this proposal, and it didn't sound remotely interesting to me. I just wanted to kick off my Sunday shoes, my white shirt and tie and my very worn out suit, and relax with some great home cooked food and a whole lot of catch up information. My mom and younger siblings, who were now getting so much bigger and grown up, just about hugged me to pieces. I had so much to talk about and so many stories to tell, and could I say something in Spanish to them? My main theme was, are there any unmarried girls left???

Once again, I felt that I had hardly sat down, when the Bishop called me to say that they had a group of Boy Scouts who were ready for Camp at Waterton Park but had no one to chaperone them, and could I take them up to camp for a week? How as a newly returned missionary could I tell them *No!!* That is how I felt under my *just got home circumstances*. But of course, I would be more than excited for the privilege. All I needed right now was to look after a group of twelve to fifteen year olds, when I hadn't even been to a store, let alone call anyone to say, "I am home!" For the most part, the boys were well behaved and having a good time. However, there are always a couple of troublemakers, and I surely knew that. Well on the third day, it was time to show them that I had been around just a bit, and I dunked them in the cold creek, clothes and all. After we got that over, we all became friends, and it was fun and games for the next several days until finally time to return home.

Arriving back home, once again, "We sure could use your help with the harvest!" Well at least that was something that I had always looked forward to, and had no hesitation to don a pair of jeans, a work shirt and a good pair of boots, and anxious to try out a self-propelled swather, a first for me. If lucky, I might even have a chance to drive a new truck or a big combine. Things had really changed in the last three years. It did feel great to be out in the fields once again doing the things that I grew up with and loved. It was a good crop, and the harvest lasted into October with little time to do much else.

Once it was over, my dad was on me again to try out the insurance business. "At least give it a try." It really wasn't so bad, but back in Raymond wasn't what I wanted, not at this stage in any event. I did take the opportunity to accept an invitation to visit with my former sweetheart, now very married, but still gorgeous, along with her mom, whom I still enjoyed. The meeting was a touch awkward considering our former relationship, but the welcome home kiss was most enjoyable, and gave me new hope to go looking for someone new. There were many stories and questions from both Janice and her mom, and I also had lots of pictures from around the globe to show.

I believed that I was now ready to spread my wings once again, and return to city life, in Calgary this time. But I did need some wheels to get around. I thought a pickup truck would do the trick, however I happened to see an ad for someone to take over a car that was about to be repossessed. It sounded like a nice unit that I should look into. Was it ever; a beautiful 1953 Mercury sedan, loaded with all the goodies. The owner was now married and couldn't finish paying for it, and I just needed to take over the payments plus a stipend to get him through. I borrowed money from the bank, a first time for me, but certainly not the last, and the car was mine. We called it "The Big M." Now ready to roll.

My father was somewhat disappointed to see me leave, but understood. He set me up with a couple of interviews with people that he was acquainted with in the insurance industry, and I was off to find my fortune or at least look for a life's companion. I didn't take the first job, but the second one as an assistant claims manager, sounded refreshing and something that I felt I could handle. It was with the Guardian Insurance Group, one of the larger insurance companies in Canada, and seemed to have a future, at least 'til I could get back on a farm.

It was now 6 months later, the spring of 1956.The pay was pretty slim, but after all, what did I know about insurance adjusting? The other personnel were all friendly and accepting of me, plus there were several pretty girls that also worked for the company. I got along fine with my immediate supervisor, and soon began to enjoy the job.

Besides a lot of desk paper work I was able to go out to check on accidents and fires and a variety of other insurance claims. Not such a bad job after all. I was boarding in one room of a boarding house with good food and owned by a nice Mormon lady. The cost was reasonable and close to work. All I had to do now was start dating once again. How do you do that when you have been away from the softer side of life for a few years? I started gingerly asking a young lady from the office for a first date. She was nice looking, and said yes right off the bat. It almost scared me, but she was very sweet and fun to be with. Unfortunately she did have a tobacco habit that didn't meet with my standards, but she did tell me, that I was about the nicest date that she had ever been with. That felt encouraging to me. It was a first date, and I knew there were a lot more choices out there. I did find that this town had lots of girls and that I couldn't possibly date them all, but it was fun trying. I had become pretty good friends with a couple of the guys from work, and we dated a variety of cute and fun gals together, driving my car mostly, because it was by far the nicest. We went to lots of movies and had lots of picnics.

One evening, another girl from the office invited me to accompany her to the party of some friends. It was a Friday evening, and I was getting a little frustrated as to where life was taking me, so I reluctantly accepted the offer. As soon as I arrived, I felt a bit nervous about the tone of the evening but thought I better stay for a while at least. There was a lot of drinking going on and I should have known better than to accept a drink from anything but an unopened can, however, was assured that it was just punch. It was just punch alright, it was laced with vodka, and I couldn't taste it, and boy did I ever get punched, completely passed out for the night. I awoke at my own apartment without my car that I dearly loved and cared for so much, and had no clue as to where it was. This girl had driven me home and then proceeded to drive to her home with my precious "Big M." She informed me that the party got really wild, and that the police had been called and advised her to get me away from there.

Oh happy day! I decided then and there that I had better step up my search for a good Mormon girl, with a good ol' pioneer background, and get married.

That incident should have cured me from any further random dating, but not quite enough to avoid any further looking around. However, I certainly became a whole lot more picky and cautious.

The three of us guys from the office dating girls from the same office made the boss a bit nervous. He said, "If you have an accident, you could wipe out an important part of our staff." He suggested that we travel in separate cars, however, that didn't happen, nor luckily neither did an accident. In thinking back about my work, I do remember a couple of spectacular claims, one that could have ended much more tragically than it did, when a couple of young boys placed a lighted firecracker in the gas spout of a neighbour's gas hauling tanker, and then ran to hide before the whole unit exploded. It sent debris scattered more than two blocks away. Our company of course paid for a new truck and tanker. The boys were frightened out of their minds, but otherwise, uninjured.

At that time, the city of Calgary was roughly 130,000 people, and not much of a swinging town for the younger population. A trip to Great Falls, Montana, was the agenda for the weekends of many of these young adults, and may be a fun thing to do. One of my friends, Doug Cassie from work, thought it sounded like a good idea for the forthcoming long weekend. I said that we could drive to Raymond after work on Friday, spend the night at my parent's home, and head to Great Falls for Saturday and Sunday. A good plan!

Of course when we arrived in Raymond, after a nice supper, my mom said, "There is a Church dance tonight, why don't you take your friend and go?" I wasn't much of a dancer and was very reluctant. Doug said "Come on, it will be fun. I have never been to a small town dance." My mother kept on encouraging me by telling me that Lizzie King's granddaughter would be there, that her grandfather had bought her a new dress, and that her cousin, Doug King was going to escort her. "Who is this girl? I don't know her."

"She lives in Calgary, is beautiful and a marvellous singer, and if you haven't met her, you must not be going to church!"

Oh, oh! Busted! "I just haven't had time, and she is probably a real dog." Well I got talked into it, and of course the first person I looked for in the dim light of the dance floor was the elusive beauty I had heard about. There she was near the door where we had entered, and wow, to my surprise, she was not only gorgeous, but had a figure that didn't quit. She was dancing with her cousin, so since I knew him well, it would be a shoe in. My friend kidded me, "I'll bet she won't dance with you!"

What a joke, of course she will. I asked her cousin to introduce me to her, and he said no. What is this? Then when I asked for a dance, she said *no!* That was not what I was used to, and it kind of hurt particularly since I had to use up a lot of nerve to ask in the first place. Then to top it all off, a fellow from Raymond whom I wasn't particularly fond of asked her and away she went.

My friend Doug had a good laugh, and then dared me to try for a date when we got back to Calgary in the next week. More things took place on Monday when we stopped at Raymond on our way back from Great Falls. As luck would have it, this girl's uncle, Bill Mehew, lived across the street from my parents and called me over from outdoors to say Hi, and to chat for a few minutes. Among other things, he said, "Have you met my niece Connie? She lives in Calgary." Then his neighbor saw us visiting and came over, "Have you met Bill's niece?" What kind of conspiracy was this, that everyone I meet suggests that I acquaint myself with this stuck-up beauty?

The neighbor even offered me to take her out in his new Buick. Sounded good, but we had to leave.

We were soon on our way back to Calgary, with more ribbing from Doug. I would have to show everyone that I would *not* be beat by this little chicky. Her name was Connie King, the granddaughter of some very prominent folks from Raymond. Her parents must be very well off. No wonder she thinks so highly of herself. I called a girl cousin of mine who also lived in Calgary, Berna Cook and she answered, "Of course I know Connie, you should take her out. I have her phone number. She is not only pretty, but is as sweet and nice as you could ever meet." Foiled once again, for sure I have to date this cutie, or never live it down.

By this time I had moved to a different apartment, a little nicer and a bit more room. With a much younger landlady, whom I could relate my story to. She told me "to get on the phone, and call her for a date, or I will do it for you!"

I didn't stand a chance. I then picked up the phone and cautiously dialled the number, almost hoping she would not be home. She did answer, and I explained who I was and had met her at a dance in Raymond, and that her Uncle Bill was our neighbor and a long-time acquaintance, and did she know my cousin, Berna Cook? Wow, I had said it. She calmly and politely said "Which one were you?"

I answered," The dark, good-looking one."

She said, "Oh yes, I remember you."

Our conversation continued as she coyly suggested the reason she turned both Doug and me down for a dance was that she saw us walk in, and thought, there's a couple of city guys that look as though they could have anyone, and if they ask me to dance, I will tell them no!

We both had a good laugh before I asked her out. Once again she said "What if I say no?," and I answered "I may not ask you again!" Her smart aleck reply was "Promise!"

Whoa, this was going nowhere. At some place in our conversation, I had stated that I had recently returned home from a church mission to Argentina, and now working in Calgary. She told me later that she had been impressed and that maybe this was it, and that she had better get off her little smart answers.

We finally made a date for the following Saturday night, and both could hardly wait for that night to arrive. Our Friday night dates that we previously had were both a washout, and were on our way to a new beginning. When I took her home that night, I asked if I might pick her up for Church meeting on the following day. She informed me that she usually went to church with another fellow to his meeting and then he would accompany her to hers. Now I was becoming the forward one when I said "Well I guess you had better make up your mind as to which direction you want to go." This was after just one date? I certainly was getting my old self-confidence back. I held my breath for her to tell me to come and pick her up, and that she would have to tell Stan that she had found a new guy.

Connie invited me in to meet her parents, and I discovered that they were far from being rich or stuffy as I had supposed. The new house that I understood they lived in was still covered with a layer of tar-paper without siding or stucco, and that it had been in that same state for several years. The inside was not yet finished either, and thus I could see that this family were a long way from being well to do. Mr. Harold King was a short stocky man with a very gruff demeanor, apparently his way to run off any suitors of his daughter. He quizzed me about my family, and didn't really seem to care for them until I informed him that my dad was Alma Hancock. He seemed to approve of him and thought that he was a pretty smart man. Connie's mother on the other hand was tall with a nice figure and pretty. I could readily see who my new found love resembled. Mrs. Melva King's maiden name was Wolsey, and was a former Cardston girl. She was really sweet and apparently very intelligent. I was very impressed with her, but for now stayed a bit clear of Mr. King, but with a determination that he wasn't going to run me off as he had done some guys in the past.

Connie and I continued to see each other almost every waking hour that we were not at work. She had been a dental assistant and recently took a job as a clerk for Imperial Oil. I continued working for the Guardian Insurance Company, being promoted, but with only a small raise in pay. We became officially engaged approximately two weeks after our first date, possibly somewhat of a record. But our attitude was, *we are in love, we are old enough, why wait?* That was on the 4th day of June 1956. Boy did I ever prove something to all of these "pushers and shovers." And I will state here and now, we did stay out of trouble and were married and sealed in the Cardston Alberta Temple in September.

I enjoyed my work, however, with a small pay cheque and now being married, I had to find an alternative job, to keep us a float and living in a nice apartment.

Wedding Bells and Babies

We were married in Cardston, Alberta, on the 29th of September, 1956. However, leading up to that, we courted since our June engagement. We spent as much time together as possible, but not without some difficulties, mostly good times, however with some challenges. As I was simply boarding in a rooming home, we could not spend time there; therefore we spent many evenings at the home of Connie's parents. This was okay with us as Mrs. King enjoyed our company, as did her younger siblings. Unfortunately Mr. King had a drinking problem, and was easily irritated. One evening he returned home from his night out, and announced to us that we could not be "roosting around in his home every evening." Of course Connie took exception to this, but he carried on his abusive tirade, telling us that should we get married, we would rue the day. I then stood up to him nose to nose with fists doubled, and announced, "We are getting married, and you cannot stop us." I then said, "Come on, Connie, let's go!"

I did not return to visit in the home until it was time for our marriage. Our evenings were spent in going to movies, church functions, or taking out a used car from a lot as a try out, and driving around the city. At Stampede time, we pooled our meagre dollars together to enter the grounds, to just walk around for the evening.

On other occasions, we drove to Raymond to visit with my family. Really, never a dull moment. At last, the day before our wedding rolled around, and I arrived at the King home to drive Connie and Mrs. King and the kids to Cardston to stay with her Grandma Wolsey. Mr. King was also there, and said "Where is everybody going?" Mrs. King simply stated, "We are going to Cardston for the marriage." Then he said "Married, who is getting married?"

"Your daughter of course!" was the answer. We then drove to Cardston where I left the family and then on to Raymond for the night. The Temple was undergoing some renovations and we were obliged to walk around paint and scaffolding to arrive to the Sealing Room for a marvellous marriage ceremony, which thus far has lasted fifty-seven-and-a half years, with more to come.

It was a strange, but joyful feeling, when we left the Temple to walk outside. There was the King family, including Harold King, Connie's father, waiting for us with open arms. Mr. King put his arms around me, and said, "Welcome to the family, son!"

I was nearly floored, but we did get along well since that time, until his passing at the age of ninety years.

We then drove to Raymond for a beautiful reception in the home of my parents, hosted by my mom and her lady friends, complete with tons of fresh flowers and a nice dinner. After the meal and many kind greetings, we scampered off on a honeymoon, first spending a night in Shelby, Montana, and then to Yellowstone Park for several more days. The weather was perfect and the park was superb.

We drove back to Calgary for another wonderful wedding reception put together this time by Connie's mother and her friends. We received many beautiful gifts, some of which we still have and use to this day.

Back to work after a couple of weeks' vacation time. I was still working for the Guardian company and Connie working at Imperial Oil. I felt that my salary would not be adequate now, and approached the big boss for a raise. He turned me down by saying, "We didn't know that you would be getting married when we hired you, so we won't pay you more."

I thought that was a very lame excuse, and began looking for alternate employment. I soon had a position with a General Insurance Agency as an Underwriter. The company was not large, but very active with a large clientele. It was owned by two older men, J.O. Miller and Bob Beasley. They were nice to work for and the staff of about a dozen were all good to get along with. There was a much homier atmosphere, and lot better wages.

I remained with this company for about one-and- a-half years, when my father called to say that his insurance business had grown to the point that he needed to hire another man to help him. He said that he sure would like me to join him, and that I could eventually become a partner and ultimately take over the ownership. The offer sounded good, and after talking it over with Connie, we both felt like we should accept, as we had become tired of city life and would welcome the chance to move to a smaller center. Our larger goal was to move to the United States, and this would be a place to work toward doing that. By the time we moved, our first son, Ricardo King Lane Hancock was born in July 1957, just ten months after our marriage. We were taken somewhat back in surprise and had a bit of a struggle adjusting to life with a family so quickly.

After living in our second Calgary basement apartment, we were ready to move on, hoping to find a nice small home in Raymond to move into. In the month of March, 1958, we packed up our belongings into the box of my father's cattle truck, covered over with a large tarpaulin, and headed to find a new and more fulfilling life in the country. To our surprise, we could not find a house to rent any place in the town. It was dead winter, and it looked as if it would be spring before anything would become available. In the meanwhile, Dad had a small one-room apartment with a half divider, in the top of his detached garage. It wasn't much, but would be a roof over our heads. Our furniture and all of our belongings sat in the back of the cattle truck in the driveway, covered with just a canvas tarp for the remainder of a cold winter. Worse than that, our small apartment was equipped with a kitchen sink only, with no toilet or shower. Night or day, it was necessary for us to walk down long stairs from the garage to outside, and then more stairs to the basement bathroom of my folk's home.

As I have said, we also had an eight-month-old baby to love and to care for. The fun and glamour was soon going out of marriage. I was working hard and spending long hours adjusting to a new occupation. My mom was sweet and understanding, but not a lot of help to my new bride and a new mother, somewhat oblivious to our needs. In any event, this was becoming a desperate strain on our fairly new marriage of less than two years. We attended our church meetings and other duties, but unfortunately being a little isolated in our living quarters, with a lot of the younger folks having moved to other parts of the country or to the USA, we had very few friends to hang around with.

We began having a few scraps because of our cramped circumstances, and although I was certainly cognizant of her feelings, I was at a loss as to how to change things until we could find a house in which to live. I was desperate, and finally located a dump of a house to move into later in the spring. At least it had a bathroom, two bedrooms, and a big yard and was warm. What more could I ask?

It was discovered by this time that Connie had a magnificent singing voice, and became extremely popular in not only our community, but other places as well. I became involved in the Chamber of Commerce and with Boy Scouts, thus our beautiful marriage soon fell back into place.

In just a few months of our living in this house, our landlord announced to us that the place had been sold, and that we would have to move next week. Luckily we found a nice one-bedroom apartment just two doors south of my office that we could move into immediately. This apartment was handy for us, but as our young son was growing fast, we looked for, and obtained a very nice two-bedroom home with a full basement. Just what we wanted to finally put down our roots and really join in with the community. We planted a garden, and some trees, and lots of flowers. The place was at last taking shape after I built a workbench in the basement, and a big sandbox outside for our son to play in. We loved the house and the location, and all of a sudden found we were expecting a second baby just about the time Ric would be three years old. Well that was wonderful, but it was a scorching hot summer, and the house was stucco. I went out every night and sprayed the house down with water to try to cool the inside a bit, as Connie was so very uncomfortable with the heat.

Our beautiful daughter Kristie was born July 20, 1960; she had lots of black hair and dark eyes. In fact the first time I saw her, the nurses had tied a big bow in her hair. Another wonderful blessing for us.

However, as our luck had been running where housing was concerned, almost two years to the day, our newest landlord came with the news, "I have sold the house, and they want to move in by the end of the month." Not a happy thought!!

We soon found a larger and nicer home that we could move into temporarily, as it was owned by a farmer who wanted to move back in late spring.

Our next home was across the street from my parents, an ideal location, just one-half block from my office, and close to church. It was owned by Connie's uncle and aunt who had moved to the United States but intended to move back in a couple of years. We rented it on that basis, and found after nearly three years, they decided to stay where they were, and sell the home.

We were ecstatic to put a mortgage together, and buy it without having to move again for years to come. It was our first very own home, and we loved it. Being homeowners, we were at last an integral part of the community. We painted everything, inside and out, and bought new carpets, drapes and bathroom fixtures. What fun we were having, even to a new lawn and trees in the back yard. Later on, we finished the basement with two bedrooms, a bathroom and large family room.

My paycheque was not large, but we were getting along. Having our own home now, a car that was paid for, our needs were not great. We fit in well with the community and our church was almost next door. We still made a few trips back to Calgary for visits with Connie's family, as well as many trips to Waterton Park. My father still owned the farm, with my brother Cal running it. I was asked to help out with harvest along with my duties in the insurance business. Once again, this was irritating to my Connie, and unfortunately the fight was on. I still loved farming and consequently enjoyed joining in with the harvest, caring for cattle, and other aspects to do with farming.

My mother, bless her heart, was always a very busy lady with Ladies Clubs, Relief Society and like things, and expected a lot from my wife along these same veins. Connie of course was not only a young wife, but also the mother of two small children. She was also a very popular singer for many funerals, weddings and church functions, and had her own agenda. My spending time on the farm along with a full scheduled business, meant that I was away many times until late evenings or at my office 'til one in the morning. Our well-oiled love machine was beginning to take a turn for the worse.

There seemed to be only two solutions, get my wife to another home further away from a busybody mother-in-law (and I say that with all due respect), or look for a different job. In my inexperienced, immature mind, *I was content*. We had a nice little home in a great location, two beautiful children, a gorgeous and talented wife, and I loved working the two jobs. The only thing I could think of that would be better was if we owned our own farm. And the last thing Connie wanted, was to live on a farm. Mainly she wasn't happy living so close to a lady that expected perfection in every move, and stated constantly "What would other ladies think?" For us, we didn't care what others thought, but knew that we had to work things out for the good of our marriage and growing family. I did understand, and took my wife's side on everything, including doing more of our own things and not being quite so involved with family.

It did work pretty well, and we decided to stay in our home. The following year was much better. I became so busy in the insurance business, and our own things that I had no more time for farm work. We had become well renowned for our insurance skills, and were obtaining clients from all over southern Alberta. We managed to have the County of Warner for our clients, which meant insuring all of the schools, school buses and roadwork equipment. We also had several semi large trucking firms insured along with hundreds of private cars and residences. To say the least, we were busy. At that time, we had the largest portfolio of business south of the city of Calgary. The Head Offices of our companies courted our firm to become our main sources. This meant longer hours at the office. However, living just a half of a block from home made it simple for me to go home for dinner or to relax at home for a couple of hours when I felt like it.

We raised a beautiful vegetable garden and lots of pretty flowers. Connie loved being out in the sunshine, as did our kids. She was a hard worker, and our home and yard became a show place.

Our second son, and third child was born in August of 1962, and named John Keith after me. One more beautiful little boy in perfect health.

At this time I was really getting involved in more church and community activities. I organized a five group Boy Scout committee that included our four LDS Wards plus the United Church. We thus became very active having group bottle drives, peanut drives, salvage drives, and at Christmas I drove a big farm truck each year to Jaffray, British Columbia, for a load of Christmas trees to sell in our town, always picking five huge ones for each Church building and an extra beautiful eleven-footer for my parent's home.

At that time the Province's Civil Defence program was coming on strong, and I was appointed Civil Defence Director for the Town of Raymond. My duties first of all, were to put an office and education program together. The town had just completed a new swimming pool and dressing rooms building and allowed me to put my classroom and office in the basement. We held classes and manoeuver exercises each week both indoors and in and out of schools, rappelling from the tops of buildings. I gained lots of followers, and travelled to a variety of communities for our practices. The threat of war was looming and some folks were even building underground bomb shelters.

Life was becoming extremely busy for us, with me getting involved in so many projects and Connie singing at most every function both in Raymond as well as neighboring towns, and our children now demanding more attention. Yet we were very happy and content with life.

Obviously my father didn't think we were busy enough, as he did love politics at any level, and became mayor of Raymond for several years during the sixties. As was always his work ethic, he became a very good mayor, achieving much for the community. He initiated the installation of natural gas in the town, paving of Main Street, and virtually putting us back on the map. This of course put a heavier load on me, and my hours of work increased once again.

We had lived in Raymond for some time now, and of course joined in with most of the current happenings. One more adventure that lasted over nine years was being asked to become part of a new male chorus. I thought when I said "yes" that it may be for a year or two, and it sounded fun. It was organized by a schoolteacher by the name of Cal Hill, who had proven himself over the years of being an excellent Choir Master. He gathered together forty men of different ages and backgrounds to form a very fine chorus. We grouped together under the name of the *Raymond Cavaliers, male chorus.* Not having a great pianist amongst the group, a very fine lady pianist was recruited, Ethyl Hicken, also from our community. She was cute, vivacious, and fun and fit right in with the all-male group. We did have an alternate pianist to fill in on occasion, Jeanine Jensen.

We practised in a church hall each Monday evening and became very professional. Our conductor, Cal Hill, knew how to extract the best out of each of us. We became well known to the point of being requested to sing at a variety of programs all over Southern Alberta, from the city of Calgary to the city of Great Falls in Montana, and most of the communities in between. We always put on a full program complete with a great Master of Ceremonies, William Love Nalder, who could keep an audience entertained by himself.

We also had quartets, duets, and solos. One guest soloist was my beautiful, talented wife Connie King Hancock. As we progressed, we dressed in a variety of styles; western with beautiful white Stetsons, tuxedoes, matching shirts and ties, etc. All very classy and in keeping with the various occasions.

Not to be out done in becoming involved in extra-curricular activities, Connie accepted not only more singing opportunities, but the chance to act in major parts of several stage plays. She became a very fine actress in these amateur productions, and enjoyed the challenge immensely. I realized now what a hum-drum life we had been living in Calgary, but were now far too entrenched in small town, to ever move back to a city, let alone the United States. Not to be stifled by work, we spent as much time as possible with our children taking many outings to the park, and to Calgary for visits with grandparents and friends. We also drove to Utah many times for other family visits or camping in Yellowstone or Zion's Canyon. Our lives were becoming pretty full, and having lots of fun.

At this time, we felt that we should perhaps do something a little more adventurous, either buy a motor home or better yet, a summer home. Neither choice felt quite right and would be far too expensive or impractical, so then what? I am not sure who came up with the idea, or if we heard someone else talking about it, but it sounded like a great adventure. We would build our own summer cottage on St. Mary's Lake in Montana.

Looking into the matter, it was feasible, and others from around our area had already done this. It would be fairly close to home, a beautiful lake, and if we shared in the work and the costs and the ownership and use of the facility, we could do it. We started by obtaining a twenty-year lease from the Indian Reserve located in Browning, Montana, on a nice piece of property next to the lake and set in a grove of aspen trees. It also had a crystal clear water spring on the edge of the large lot. Perfect for drinking water and giving us a name for our new cottage, "Spring Dell Cottage." It would be owned by myself and Connie, my brother Cal and wife Lynn, and our parents, Al and Ella.

We commenced immediately with a three-bedroom design, a solid concrete foundation, studs and plywood flooring, walls and roof. We also designed a large kitchen and sitting room. The next item was a very large deck for lounging, barbeques and in general for entertaining lots of family and friends. We then built a boat dock for our proposed future boat.

Camping in a tent while building, we were all ready to go for many years of family fun.

On December 28th, 1966, our fourth and last child was born. Another beautiful daughter, Lisa Jill, full of life, and ready to meet the world. We were not sure how that came about, as we had wanted to have one more child for the past two or three years to add to our growing family. She was truly a welcome blessing and a belated Christmas gift to us. I believe that we finally discovered the secret.

Each of our children were born healthy and strong, a wondrous blessing from God. I must also give credit and awe to their beautiful mother, my sweetheart wife, Connie. I love you so much and admire womanhood more than I can tell.

Now in January of 1971, my father was involved in a very serious car accident that nearly took his life. He spent much time in hospital, leaving him crippled to the point that he was required to retire from active business life, leaving me to take over a growing and almost life consuming business.

Surprisingly, in July of 1972, we were approached by two brothers from Utah, former Cardston men, who decided to return to Canada with their families to make their homes. They were impressed with what they saw, and made us a good offer, wanting to take over sometime in August.

I had two very capable secretaries that knew the business well, and were willing to stay on. One had been with me for fourteen years, and coincidently was the aunt of the wife of one of these young men. Everyone was happy, and I was elated and relieved for the change, though I had grown to love the business. My father was not well, and after twenty years at this occupation, was more than ready.

Life all of a sudden was becoming a whirlwind of activity. A month or so earlier, we had taken delivery of a brand new station wagon automobile that we ordered from the factory, and had started planning a trip to Disney Land in convoy with Cal and Lynn and our families. Things came together very quickly now. They had a new Camper, and we pulled a small trailer, camping as we travelled. Our kids were almost the same ages, and we had a safe and grand time.

When in the United States, we travelled over to the State of Oregon, and then along the coastal highway. On one camping stop, we allowed our ten-year-old boys to walk down to the beach to play in the sand as well as take a dip for the first time in the ocean. During their time there, a dark cloud came overhead along with a very strong wind, almost blacking out any visibility. Of course we were concerned for the boys' safety, and began hollering and searching frantically for them. Not being familiar with the area, we also lost our way looking for them. Fortunately the wind quieted and the cloud moved off and we found them okay, but all of us were very frightened.

The next couple of days camping found us being much more

cautious. However, reaching San Francisco in the evening, we drove down what we thought would take us directly back to the main highway. It eventually did, but first took us down a well-lit and busy street of Night Clubs, Discos, and Ladies of the Night, showing off their wares. We hoped the kids would be asleep. Not so, the boys were laying on the overhead bunk in the camper with a perfect view of all of the action. They admitted to it several days later.

We arrived at a nice campground near Disney Land a day later, and spent a wonderful three days going on almost every ride and show in the park. Before returning home, we travelled to Mexico for an additional two days. We didn't go far into this country, but far enough to view a lot of poverty and slum type living. We and our kids were happy to return home and quite content to live in small town Raymond, at least for the present.

Lots of Changes

NO LONGER OWNING A BUSINESS, NOR EVEN HAVING A JOB, I WAS talked into accepting the nomination as a candidate to run for Member of Parliament for the Federal Social Credit Party in the forthcoming 1972 Election. This would be for the Constituency of Warner, which included the City of Lethbridge, the towns of Cardston, Pincher Creek, Fort Macleod, Picture Butte and Warner, plus many other smaller communities. I didn't start out as a politician, but after a few weeks of heavy campaigning, I was doing pretty well. I was interviewed on radio, television and by a variety of newspaper persons.

Competing in community hall debates, schools and universities, I was almost beginning to enjoy the limelight and attention I was getting. Along with several well-known personalities of our area, my sweetheart, Connie, accompanied me throughout my entire campaign. When all was over and the smoke cleared, I lost the fight, but did a good job, and showed well. After my television interview to thank all of my supporters, I drove to the winner's victory party, and found him so drunk that he could scarcely stand up. It was sad and disgusting to see who our constituents voted in. As most found later, he did about the same in office. People in our area wanted the Trudeau Government out of office so badly, I believe they would have voted in anyone of the Conservative Party. This was my first and last fling at politics, but all in all, was a great experience. Well, I did have one other small foray into the political scene. I was elected to the school board and served one term. That was enough politics for me.

The Realities of Real Estate

I WAS NOW NOT ONLY TIRED, BUT COMPLETELY UNEMPLOYED AND with a growing family knew that I needed to get busy working again. My brother Cal was now not only farming, but was selling "packaged houses" as well as constructing them. I went to work with him until May of 1973 when I decided I had to get serious with a new occupation. I felt that Real Estate may be my niche, and checked out several companies in Lethbridge, settling on a career with Hay Realty, later to become Time Realty. I enjoyed the challenge, and worked hard to prove myself, and helped to put the company in number one position in Southern Alberta. I worked mostly in the Raymond market, and in the following few years, had sold forty percent of the homes in our town, along with many farms. Not to elevate myself more than I should but I did in one year, sell more properties than the nine other realtors in our office put together. My steadfast work paid off, and I gained a good reputation as a realtor with farm sales to clients from Germany and Italy as well as locally.

I well remember one of my very first sales. I had not yet purchased a business car, and drove an El Camino pick-up truck to work. It was pretty and new but was small inside, having but the one seat. Two very tall men came into the office on my floor day, looking to buy an acreage close to Lethbridge, I had just listed what I thought they were looking for, near Stirling, about twenty miles to the south. I offered to show it to them, not giving a thought to my vehicle. When we got to the parking lot to get in, I discovered that both who were approximately six-and-a-half feet tall, had to sit with their knees right under their chins, jammed in like sardines. I thought to myself "Well so much for that sale." However much to my surprise they rode with me harmoniously, and paid cash for the acreage without questioning the price. Talk about my gaining confidence in selling real estate!!

I very soon bought a four-door sedan for business after that experience.

Not only was my newfound occupation treating me well, but it was beginning to be a lot of fun with many humorous experiences along the way with earning an extra good living. One problem with the sales type of business, it does have many ups and downs, and as said about real estate. "It is chicken one day, and feathers the next." I learned rather quickly about one of the more fun parts. I had become quite close to the owner/manager of Time Realty and to his very good friend, the bank manager, when they invited me to attend the local horse races with them. I knew horses quite well, and thought it would be fun as well as a prestige thing to do. Looking the horses over, I placed a small bet on one; it came in first! I won eight dollars! Wow, was I good. I successfully did this a couple more times, winning a small amount each time, as did my friends. I got a little braver with a twenty dollar bill, but I lost it. I was up about five dollars and said to myself, "That's it!" I haven't bet on another horse in all these many years.

The owner of the company became ill in 1975, and requested that I take over the management for a short time, and become a partner to him later. We never did come to proper terms before he confessed to me that he had overspent and asked if I could temporarily bail him out. As we had become good friends, I signed some bank notes with him, which I discovered later, that he and his banker had not disclosed some important facts to me, ultimately forcing me to pay off thousands of dollars of his debts.

This put me in a financial bind that took me several years to pay off. Despite my trying, my friend and his wife both became alcoholics, rejecting help from both Connie and myself.

I was still trying to keep Time Realty afloat not withstanding my setback and disappointment in my friend, when another personal friend of mine, a well to do farmer from the Warner area, Howard Hamling, approached me to list and sell a large portion of his grain farm, and in turn he would buy another large property that was closer to his home place. It would sell for a lot of money, and would take a special buyer to handle it. In the meantime, I had a good client from Germany whom I felt would be interested, and could certainly handle it financially. Upon contacting him, I found that he would be in Ontario in a few weeks, and could we meet with him there. My friend Howard and I decided to fly to Toronto to meet with him and his partners to try to put the deal together. We did so with some success, spending about ten days there, and also making several other good contacts. Unfortunately, just as we were putting a deal together, the Canadian government came up with a retroactive ban on selling large tracts of farm land to any and all foreign buyers unless they intended to physically move onto the land itself within one year of purchase. This would not be the case with my buyers, as it was being purchased strictly as a future investment. After consulting with our lawyers, the deal fell through before we returned home.

I later opened my own successful business in Raymond, and sadly, Time Realty went under.

My new business opened under the name of Hancock Land Real Estate Corp Ltd, and operated from a small commercial building located in the heart of the business district. It consisted of a front reception area and two offices plus a washroom. It had formerly been a barbershop for many years. As I had previously renovated this building for an office, the transition was easy. I was currently working with the people in Raymond for their real estate needs, and was well known and respected. I had also sold a number of farms in the past, however, felt that a full time farm sales person would be an asset to me. I had just looked out of the front window with this thought in mind, when an older farmer friend of mine walked by. I knew that he had recently turned his farm to his son to operate and was probably thinking of something else to work at. His name was Willard Paxman. He had been a very successful farmer, was about fifteen years my senior, and had in fact been my contemporary in the Federal Election, with the same result as me. I thought, "Perfect!"

I called him in, "Just what I was hoping for," said he. We began working together making a great combination for both the sale of residential properties, businesses and farms. I was being very blessed and now feeling much more secure in my decision to become a business man rather than a farmer or rancher. Together we were wrapping up almost all of the sales in the area, and could not keep up with the work.

We were not only in need of another salesperson, but were in need of a larger office. Another unexpected blessing, just at that very time, the Bank of Montreal who owned the large building right next door to mine, became available. They had just completed a new office across the street and were moving in a few days. I hurried and put some finances together and grabbed it up before anyone else had the opportunity. It was just right for us, in size, location and condition. Moving in was a breeze. We had to do very little to fit it to our business, and could in fact accommodate several more sales people as needed. I did hire two more people, a much-needed secretary, and a young woman sales person. We all worked together well, and meeting our clients requirements as well as our own.

In March of 1975, my father had completed a new home next door to his present large home. The beautiful older home was simply much too big for my mom to care for, and my father was not in proper health to take up the slack. Their desire was to keep it in the family, and requested Connie and me to purchase it from them as they were ready to move next door into their newly constructed home. My brother Cal was the contractor, and with some help from the family, built a smaller beautiful home for Dad and Mom to move into.

For some strange reason, we didn't jump at the chance, thinking that we would simply build an addition on to our existing place. I knew a good builder, and he had drawn up some very favourable plans for an add on. The home of our folks was sitting on two acres was huge and, was at that time, fifty years old, but in beautiful condition. We simply didn't even want to consider the move. I am not sure to this day why we altered our decision, but as I think back on it, it was almost the best decision of our lives, standing next to our marriage and our wondrous kids (well most of the time).

I approached all of my siblings before buying the home to find out if any of them wanted the opportunity to buy it. They all stated a definite *No*! As things worked out, my younger brother who at the time was teaching and living in Taber, Alberta, had recently purchased the newspaper business in Raymond, wanted to buy our home and move here. Once more, not just a coincidence, but a very timely blessing for each of us. We all moved basically in one day, hiring movers for Bert's family to move from Taber, and the others of us along with the moving men, carried things next door to my parent's home, and across the street from our home to our new home. We have never had a moment of regret in these nearly forty years. Obviously making it a permanent home for Connie and me and our family. It is getting old and has been declared an *Historic Home*, but is still beautiful and we love it.

About this time, I was voted to become a member of the Board of Directors on the Lethbridge Real Estate Board, which covers all of Southern Alberta. I became Chairman of the Ethics Committee and later First Vice President. I served as a Director for five years, having the opportunity of not only being an advisor to our own board members, but to travel to wonderful conventions held each year in all parts of Canada, from Victoria to Montreal.

In our own business we continued on an upward swing, adding several more sales people to our staff. With luck and good fortune in these years, I received many awards and accolades for my service.

In these first few years of moving into our new building, I had four sales people along with myself, and a full time secretary under our roof, all doing quite well and earning a decent living.

Having so recently been Working in the Lethbridge market, I was still getting calls to list and sell homes in the city. One sunny afternoon as I sat at my desk, I received a call from a lady who said she had seen one of my signs on a property in Lethbridge that she would like to look at. Of course I obliged by making an appointment to show this home. When I drove up to the house, I saw that there were three very striking looking ladies standing in front waiting for my arrival. Their car was new and expensive, and they all three were dressed to the nines. I thought to myself, this looks promising. When I alighted from my car, all of a sudden, I felt and heard my slacks rip open at the seam from top to bottom. What could I possibly do? I was there, they were there. My appointment had been made. I showed the house very hurriedly, backing up all of the way, away from them. I can't remember of ever being so embarrassed or intimidated. They were all three about the classiest ladies I had ever shown properties to, and I didn't even try to sell them, I just wanted to get out of there.

It was during these better times, that we managed to send our eldest son, Ricardo, to the Brigham Young University for one year prior to fulfilling a two-year mission for the Church in New York City, which of course was an expense directly out of our own pocket. By this time, our eldest daughter, Kristie Lee, had graduated from high school with excellent grades and was also raring to attend the Brigham Young University. This we were overjoyed to oblige.

Sadly enough, as with many farms and businesses, real estate sales began to taper off after a boon of prosperity for several years, and I found it necessary to borrow more and more from the bank to help my business and employees to exist. When listings came in, I had a tendency to turn them over to one of my sales people rather than keep them for myself, thus keeping my staff going. We were still on the leading edge of the industry, however, times were heading for a great fall. People who had homes were holding on to them, and those without a home could not or *did not* want to take a chance on losing one if they did buy. Interest rates also played a big part in the economy, sky rocketing up to 18 and 20 percent for a mortgage. Was it any wonder that our businesses were plummeting? I remember walking out of the front door one morning, briefcase in hand, and turning to my loving wife, and saying to her, with tears in my eyes, "Where do I think I am going?" The phone was not ringing, no one was coming in the door, and the bank manager just gave me a side glance when I stopped in there. I was beginning to feel like I had dropped off the planet. I was broke and didn't know it. Having a little extra time on my hands, I felt like I needed to fill in with some other type of business. I had become quite proficient at appraising homes and acreages, and had been approached by several financial institutions to do regular appraisals for them. I didn't have the proper credentials for appraising, but I did have the skills. At that time, the banks didn't really care as long as they had something in writing. This I did, and ended up doing appraisals for fourteen different banks and/or credit lending institutions. I was very thorough with my inspections, and did a good job on writing up my reports along with pictures and diagrams. They were all happy and paid me well, and I was making the extra money I needed to keep going. Along with this and my sales, I began handling rentals for absentee owners of about thirty properties. All of these things kept me busy until interest rates began to drop, and sales started to pick up once again.

More Family

THE CHURCH IMPLEMENTED A PLACEMENT PROGRAM OF NATIVE children to live and attend school in our area for the school term. We were asked to participate in this program, and did so for two years. We had a young man fourteen years of age John Anthony Yorke, from the Queen Charlotte Islands come live in our home, and integrated in with our own children. The program was to give these children an opportunity to become better educated in both schooling and life away from poor living conditions at their homes on the reserves across North America. The kids' families were happy for this program that was put in place in Canada and the United States. It was very successful in many places, but a failure in others, to the point that it only lasted two years.

We very much enjoyed having Tony, as we called him, live with us for the two years, and seemed to work quite well, as he did return home where he afforded himself with more education, married well and had two beautiful daughters who deemed Connie and me to be Grandma and Grandpa, even to this day. We have visited them in their nice home in Metlakatla, B.C., and they have visited with us in our home in Raymond.

Our visit to their home was our first so far north on land, and proved to be very enjoyable. We had no idea as to what to expect, whether we would stay in a tent, a log cabin or a house. They had a very lovely split-level home. Tony had a nicely set up shop in his garage where he did carvings and created other interesting items to sell. The village could not be reached by land because of the spongy marsh like land, so we had to travel by boat to get to Metlakatla from Prince Rupert. I was somewhat nervous about leaving my car in a parking lot, however I was assured by Tony that it would be safe and untouched.

The village area was totally fascinating. The sounds of large birds echoed through the trees as we traversed the beautiful ground covered marshlands. We also walked the beach picking up clams that the peoples used for clam bakes, and boated to an island where ancient cultures were displayed. We ate very well while there, and watched in dismay as the young people of the village ran to meet the fishing boats as they arrived with their catch, and went right to work cleaning and/or eating parts of the raw fish. Susan, being a nurse, received phone calls all hours in the night as also the day to help someone in distress. Also while visiting the family, Tony did a native dance for us using a gorgeous handmade blanket with hundreds of hand sewn buttons representing the cultures of the whale. He later presented the blanket to us as a precious gift. It was a wonderful visit and certainly a cultural eye opener for us. The following summer, the family travelled to our home for a visit. The girls told us that the thing they missed the most was their seaweed which they dried and ate like we eat potato chips. Not my delicacy, but they loved it. We have not been in touch with them very often in these past several years, but still feel love for one another, talking on the phone occasionally.

A New Phase

Our son, Ric (Ricardo), had returned to university soon after his mission where he met a beautiful young lady by the name of Sheri Price, from Parowan Utah, and began a serious courtship. He called home just before Christmas to say that he was bringing her home to spend Christmas with our family, if that would be okay. Of course this was exciting and certainly a new adventure for our family to anticipate perhaps a forthcoming marriage.

They arrived a few days before Christmas and as we watched from our dining room window as they drove up, the ground was covered with deep snow and beautiful light snow falling. The picture was perfect as they alighted from their car. We could see that she had long blond hair, matching her snow- covered attire perfectly. Ric, the gentle person that he is, was helping her with every footstep through the deep snow. Christmas music was playing softly, our home was decorated complete with tree and lots of festive colored lights inside and out, which also enhanced this stunning picture. No movie could have depicted this scene more eloquently nor thrilled our family more. It appeared this young lady would be the first new addition to a loving family, with the excitement of many more to follow in due time. Now to make this season complete, we just needed our sweet Kristie Lee to also arrive from university in a couple of days.

I had not seen her in four months, and was so very excited to have all of our family together for the first time in two years. The other kids had made a large sign of "Welcome Home Kristie." The Christmas season has always been so very special to each of us, and having Sheri join us was extra special for the family. After a few days, we just knew that wedding bells were in the air, and would not be too long from now. With Ric having been on a mission for the past two years, we knew this would turn out to be our most memorable Christmas yet, and it was.

Not only did the love and excitement flow, but each person did something special. Connie was in charge of the ward choir, and planned a special cantata for the 24th. She had practised and worked on this for the last two months, and was it ever beautiful, a memorable treat for the entire congregation. Ric, who is a great songwriter, composed and sang several special numbers. Lisa, who at age eleven is also a phenomenal singer, indescribable unless one has heard her, sang several songs for the family. John K. at age 16, standing extra tall, had made all of his fine gifts in woodworking shop. He had also made an extra finely crafted table lamp for his own home someday, unselfishly presented it to Ric and Sheri. On top of it all, Ric did in fact present an engagement ring to his love. Many, many other special events took place during this very once in a lifetime Christmas.

After such a high, it is difficult to have the kids return back to university, however there is usually something to get us back on track. A couple of months later, our sweet Lisa Jill invited me to take her on a "Daddy Daughter" date. Wow, another very special event. She had on a sweet new dress, fixed her own hair beautifully, complete with a flower in it, and looked absolutely radiant. All of the ward class members performed a special number on the program, Lisa sang "My Dear Earthly Father" to me, as only she can do. It is hard for people to imagine such a voice from someone so young. It was magnificent. We ate, we danced, we had some good laughs, we took pictures. When we returned home she excitedly reported the evening to her mom, then said, "I wonder what I would have said in a talk instead of singing?"

She then disappeared to her room, and a half hour later, returned with the most beautiful poem dedicated to me, "A Tribute to My Father." Once again, tears flowed freely. Lisa has always been *our sunshine girl*, and has brought so much joy and brightness to our lives.

Our eldest son, Ricardo King Lane Hancock, and new bride Sheri Lynn Price, were married February 17, 1979 in the Cardston, Alberta Temple. The marriage was originally scheduled for April 27th, which we felt didn't allow much time to prepare. However, as it turned out, a desperate call came, stating that they had to move it up to February. Sheri had entered a poem in a Bridal Contest in Salt Lake City, and Ric had put music to it, and they had won the contest. There was to be a faux wedding held in the Salt Palace, with all of the trimmings from a variety of merchants, a huge reception in the Salt Palace with pictures by a professional photographer, wedding gown for the bride and her party and tuxedos for the groom and his men. The prize also included a stay at a luxurious hotel, a trip to Acapulco Mexico, topped off with a stay at Disney Land, just too much to turn down; but they had to conform to the date set by the Bridal Contest. If we felt we were being rushed before, we really had to press forward with this new turn of events. We of course also planned a wedding and reception for them here before the Salt Lake occasion. One down and three to go, but not too soon we hope.

I may have made that statement too soon. Our daughter Kristie Lee, as I have mentioned, was also attending university at the BYU, with no thought of marriage, so far as we knew. However, as one might guess, showed up with a beautiful ring. Before I passed out, she quickly reported that it was just a promise ring, and that the young man, Alan Pitt, would be going on a mission soon, and she would have two years ahead of her.

I was somewhat relieved with this information, however still had some doubts. She was nearly nineteen, beautiful and smart, and who knows what may happen at BYU?

In the meantime, our stake was about to put on a stage play, and had asked Connie to take one of the leading roles, which meant a lot of practises. The one bright spot was they also gave our youngest daughter a part in the play, that of the leading soloist in the starting of the production. They both spent many hours in practise in the following months. The production was called "Saturday's Warrior." The seats were sold out quickly, and it was viewed by more than four thousand people. Both Connie and Lisa received tremendous reviews, and were absolutely awesome. Lisa sang the solo part to start the production and then another for the finale. She was also asked to perform at a special concert held in Lethbridge later on, singing the same songs. At age eleven, she was unsurpassed.

With summer approaching, we were busy getting our yard in shape for any visitors that might show up, and especially for July First, our town parade and Stampede celebration days. We always put a beautiful float in the parade each year, and have won first prize in more than twenty five years. Connie does most of the decorating, and puts a new theme in every year. She has sat on the hood of the car or truck in a bathing suit most of the years, perhaps that won us first prize. Our daughters have been on them some years. Like their mom, they are also both beauties. We have until the last two years, had what we call a "driveway party" after the parade, inviting family and friends for a potluck lunch. We have had as many as 130 at one time. On occasion people that knew none of us also showed up to eat. No problem, everyone was welcome. Our lawn next to the busy sidewalk running in front of the house was always lush and green, with strangers sitting out on a blanket eating their lunch. Our home being a Provincial Historic location, we are always happy to share with curious or interested persons.

This particular summer, our son John, decided he was due to work elsewhere for the summer rather than home, and found employment at Banff Park, pumping gas at a Lake Louise Shell station. It was said to be the busiest station in Canada in the summer, with a non-stop steady stream of cars. It was hard work, but he was paid well and enjoyed getting away from Raymond for a change. He was voted High School President that year, and felt he deserved a bit of a vacation from his home town.

Kristie also showed up with Alan Pitt for a couple of weeks before summer semester, and enable the family to get better acquainted with Alan. Later in the summer, Alan did get a mission call to Seoul, Korea, and Kristie flew down to Odessa, Texas, for his farewell.

Real estate sales finally picked up and I had an extremely busy summer with balancing my time doing that, spending time with family at home and getting in two or three vacation trips. It felt so good to at last have a bit of extra money to spend, a luxury that we had not had for a few struggling years. The old adage of *make hay while the sun shines* definitely applied in my business, and that is what I tried to do, but still take as much family time as I possibly could. I love life!!

Having a Texan join our family just didn't seem to be in the cards. I just got through talking about Alan Pitt, who at this time was still on a mission, when receiving an exciting but somewhat confusing phone call from our university student, Kristie Lee, announcing that she was engaged to be married. But how was this possible when Alan was not yet home? Well it wasn't to Alan, but to one John J Fisher of California. Before I could get any of my objections out, she quickly informed us that he was a returned missionary, and not only that, but that he had served in Argentina, my former stomping grounds. Well, what could I say after that news? He couldn't be all bad! My Connie and I had never made it a habit to interfere too much in the lives of our growing children. They had been taught well, and to pray about their important decisions, and if they felt right about something pertaining to their own lives of this magnitude, go for it. But of course after our *congratulations*, I had to throw in a "Are you sure" and a "What about Alan?" However to no avail, the decision had been made, and of course he was just the greatest. Not to lengthen this out, he was and is a wonderful man, and after more than 30 years and five sons later, we love him to pieces.

In looking back over this bizarre story, I find that I neglected to mention a fine little book that my beloved Connie wrote and had published. It is called "How Well Do You Know Me?" It is about all of the Prophets of the Church, up to and including Spencer W. Kimball. It went over well, and was a very enjoyable read. She sent a copy to several General Authorities, and received some very favourable personal letters back, including one from President Kimball and Marion G. Romney and others.

One of these books went to Father O'Reilly, our local Catholic priest, as well as to many of his parishioners. It became a hot topic at the start, however, Father O'Reilly became acquainted with us and we three became good friends. He even invited Connie to sing at three of his midnight Christmas Masses. Against some objections from his congregation, she sang "O Holy Night" as well as "Ave Maria"; wherein he told them that he liked it and would have it sung if he wanted to. On our wedding anniversaries, he would send us beautiful bouquets of flowers along with a nice card. We remained very good friends right up to his death from cancer, visiting with him just hours before he passed.

After several months' courtship between Kristie Lee and John J, we had another beautiful wedding on our hands. Once again in the Cardston, Alberta Temple, with a wonderful family dinner held at the famous Cobblestone Restaurant after the marriage.

A garden reception was to be held at our home in early evening in the backyard where we had spent many hours preparing for the occasion with every blade of grass trimmed and every leaf in just the right place. However the higher powers that be had other plans, our once bright blue skies turned black the day before the wedding and did we ever get a good two day soaking. The grounds still looked immaculate and wonderful for pictures the following day. Many family, friends and acquaintances showed up regardless of the weather, and we all had a great time with this beautiful couple whom I think were oblivious to the weather. They had decided to make their home in California for the summer and then return to Provo in the fall to complete their schooling. As John and his family were from Canyon Country, California, another reception was to be held there in a week's time. Ric and Sheri and baby lived in California at this time and did not come home for the wedding, as they knew that our complete family would be coming down for this reception. This took place in June of 1981, and the remainder of summer was sunny and hot, perfect for vacationing. We enjoyed meeting John's family and friends, and spent much time with our own kids, visiting, eating and time on the beautiful beach, and getting to know our new little grandson, Ben Jamin (called "Jamin"), who was now one year old.

Ric now had employment with a record producing company as manager of one of the several departments. Music is the love of his life (next to family of course), and this job was exactly what he had hoped for when moving to this state. It was enjoyable and very enlightening to see how vinyl records are produced. He was in charge of quality, stamping out the discs, and overseeing the covers that encase the final product. Ric had also got a small band together, working toward a new future.

With our two eldest children now married and living away from home, even though they have spent much of their time at university, our home seemed more empty than ever, and time for a new project. Our second son, John Keith, was now at the age to consider a Church mission, and looked forward to a call. His birthday wasn't until the middle of August, but was anxious for an interview to get started.

John's mission call finally arrived with all of the excitement on November 21st, my mom's birth date. He was called to the Arizona Holbrook Mission and was scheduled to enter the Mission Training Center on January 14th, 1982. This was a very exclusive mission, having to learn and speak the Navajo language. It was a relatively small mission, for one reason, the language was very hard to learn, and the peoples had a difficult time accepting the Gospel. John continued to be thrilled with his call, and after two months in the training center, learned the language quickly and was eager to get started. He told us that one of the most difficult situations was having to retrieve a drunk Branch President out of jail on various Sundays, and literally carry him to the church for meetings.

Meanwhile back at home, Lisa Jill, as Kristie had previously done, worked for me doing secretarial work in my office. It not only gave the girls good experience, but they were both expert at the job, and saved me from needing to hire another lady for several different months. We enjoyed working together during those months. Mostly they handled our clients with their rental concerns.

Once again interest rates soared into the twenty percentages and sales dropped off. Our federal government, under the leadership of Pierre Elliot Trudeau, was taking a heavy toll on the country's economy, seemingly leading us rapidly into communism, and financial ruin. This may be my opinion, however, it was shared by most westerners, with the thoughts of separating from eastern Canada. Not a wonderful situation, but becoming a very popular consideration.

We did have an enjoyable Christmas again this year, with all of the kids home, with the addition of Sheri and one-and-a-half year old Jamin, and John J, Kristie's husband. How fun was it for me to take my new little grandson down town to see Santa, and look at the many toys.

We were into the year of 1982, and hopefully a great one. John now in the mission field was doing fantastic, and had been very faithful at writing to us each week. It was a good mission for him to be in, communicating with native people, and being out in open country, which he has always loved. The weather was hot and he was also free to help the people repairing houses and cars etc., another love.

We enjoyed being grandparents so very much, and now received some double enjoyable news, we would not only become new grandparents once again, but twice in the coming of June. Sheri and Ricardo were expecting their second, and Kristie and John J were expecting number one. We didn't know yet if they would be boys or girls, or perhaps one of each but will be very close in age. Connie was anxious to go to both Utah and California to be with both girls, so was hoping there would be a few weeks in between their births. Lisa would also like to go to California for the summer to work on music with her brother Ric, and of course to tend Jamin while Sheri is in hospital.

One more important event before baby time. Connie enrolled in an eight week, once-a-week, art class. She has always been a terrific sketch artist, but felt like she would love to do oil painting as well, or in place of. Her first oil painting was that of our son John while still in the mission field and taken from a photo. It turned out marvellous, and the start of one more talented career, with dozens more to come over the next thirty years. What a wonderfully talented girl, singer, artist, writer and teacher and *beautiful*. How lucky, or fortunate was I to follow others advice to find and marry her.

Reading from my journal dated May 23rd, 1982, I wrote: "I am sitting alone in this great big home, wishing to be elsewhere with some of my family. However, that won't be for at least another two weeks. Last week I took both Connie and Lisa to Utah. Lisa flew from there to California to spend the summer with Ric, Sheri and Jamin.. ... As Kristie is expecting her first little baby any day now, Connie remained in Utah with Kris and John until after the baby is born, and for a week or so after.

Consequently I am back home and very much alone. Since our marriage, Connie and I have been fortunate enough to not be apart for more than about ten days at one time, and this time will be at least three weeks. If Sheri has her baby within a week or so after Kristie, Connie may very well fly direct to California. Spring finally arrived a bit late in good ol' Southern Alberta with some beautiful days. Yesterday I planted our large garden, which was a first for me."

I have helped plant every year, but have never planned or planted alone. That was always one more of Connie's projects. It was enjoyable to watch it take shape, and I even drew a coloured map of the outlay afterwards. Saturday I mowed all of the lawns, watered everything, and had the whole yard looking fantastic.

As things turned out, our second handsome grandson, John J Fisher III (called "J") was born on June 9th, to John J and Kristie Fisher in Utah. Ric and Sheri had not yet had their little one so Connie returned home with my nephew and family. What fun it was to greet her on a gorgeous sunny day, the house sparkling clean, patio and drive swept, and the lawns and garden looking so fantastic. I wasn't sure what time they would arrive, so I got up early to start the day, having all in readiness for her arrival. After being gone for thirty-five days, it was as though we had been apart for years rather than just a month. I love her so much, she truly is *my Queen!*

On the 22nd of the month, our first granddaughter, Shelsi Tenille Hancock, was born to Ric and Sheri in Burbank, California. Of course both Connie and I were anxious to leave for California almost immediately; Lisa was still there. Shelsi, like her mom, was beautiful, blonde and had brown eyes. Now we had both genders. We spent a couple of weeks there before returning to Raymond, and were able to be there for Shelsi's blessing. Speaking of blessings, what a wonderful blessing this beautiful new little soul was that just joined our family.

This was not my intention to write from my journal, but I feel to take the liberty of repeating a page or so from December 1982: "The year 1982 is drawing quickly to a close. I could say that I am glad that it is nearly over as it has been another financially trying year, the second in a row, but why look on the gloomy side? Actually it has been a very rewarding and exciting year. What could be more fulfilling than to start a year with a good and faithful son going into the mission field with a strong and exciting testimony of the Gospel and an equal amount of enthusiasm and energy to match? What could be more fulfilling than to start the summer off with not one but two brand new arrivals fresh from Heaven in the form of another grandson and a soft little granddaughter, both strong, healthy, and beautiful? What could be more fulfilling than a great summer vacation visit with a family that you love so much? What could be more fulfilling than to receive so many testimony building letters from a hard working missionary son who has learned to love and to care for the Indian people he is living and laboring with; to share his sorrows and feel with him the joys of success? What could be more fulfilling than to watch a beautiful garden grow and take shape, reach maturity and yield a fruitful harvest? What could be more fulfilling than to see the year drawing to a close with the love of your life, my dear Connie, having gained near perfection in a new found talent in completing a fantastic oil portrait of all of our six children and her husband (me), as well as a portrait of Sister Camilla Kimball, to be presented to President and Sister Kimball, as well as a wonderful portrait of a precious little deceased eight year old girl whose very spirit and soul was captured on canvas. And yes, what could be more fulfilling than to have a dear Celestial like family loving and living the Gospel principles and looking forward to spending Christmas together in John J and Kristie's little apartment in Utah and closing off the year of 1982 as a united family, and dedicating ourselves to a new and fulfilling year to come in 1983? We were not without our share of cares and worries and heartaches in 1982, but I am ever grateful to my Heavenly Father for His love and goodness to me and the family I love with every fibre of my being. And John, my son, wherever you are in the mission field, that *includes* you!"

One of our first concerns of the New Year came about in February, when my mom became very ill, and had to be taken to hospital by Connie. She did rally somewhat from her illness, enough that family and friends were able to visit with her for a couple of more months off and on, but she never regained her full health and strength.

For a short time it looked as though she would be okay, allowing us the opportunity for me to fill a business commitment in Idaho. I was broker for a Time Share company headquartered in Stone Ridge, Idaho, and scheduled to do a seminar for the salespeople on May 2nd, thus we were still there until May 8th, our day to leave for home, when a call came that mom had just passed away. It was also Mother's Day, a very fitting day for her to be called home. She was only seventy-four years, but had been in poor health for quite some time and was suffering much. We had so recently spent some beautiful time with her, feeling of her love and concerns for the entire family, and each of us felt it a blessing for her to go.

She had been a teacher for young women for many years as well as a Relief Society president for years, which gave her many loving fans. The funeral was one of the largest held in our community because of her popularity, and of course was especially beautiful with flowers and tributes by the dozens. Being Mother's Day made it more special for our family.

The death of our mom was extremely difficult for dad, but with a very loving family, he would be okay.

With my mother now being gone and my father in poor health and extremely lonesome for her, life had taken on quite a different twist. Living next door, and having worked so closely with my dad for so many years, he seemed to be very dependent on me for nearly everything. I almost desperately needed something else to occupy any spare time that I had. Fortunately this year of 1983 so far had new life come to my sluggish business; I was busy! Like I have stated before, the real estate business seems to be boom or bust, and I never know from one month to the next how it is going to go for the year. I was writing up offers and closing deals, nearly two per week! I was also busy with my appraisal business, which sort of goes hand in hand with sales.

To top this off, in April I was approached by a good friend, Bruce Harvey, to start a used appliance business as a side line. With my own business having slowed down in the past, I agreed that it may fill in a few gaps for us. Bruce was an excellent appliance repairman, and knew the business already, and also loved to attend auctions to bid on used units. We formed a partnership and found a small empty commercial building on Main Street to get started. Every Tuesday and Thursday evenings, there was an auction in Lethbridge that we could attend to purchase used appliances that seemed to be in good shape. If they needed a little repair work, Bruce put them in excellent working condition, we then cleaned them up and sold them at very reasonable prices. It did keep us very busy, and we were making a decent profit, as well as having a lot of fun going to auctions, or buying from ads in the newspaper. We worked well together and cemented an already good friendship to an even closer one. I basically kept the books.

Our son John, who had been called to the normal two-year Church mission, happened to get caught in a temporary change of policy to an eighteen-month term. He was not excited with the change, nor were his mom and I. However, we had no choice in the matter and he therefore finished at the end of June. We made the decision to travel to Arizona to bring him home, and packed the car up for a lengthy trip on July 4th. Our daughter Lisa, travelled with us, making the trip even more enjoyable. We drove straight through to Utah, staying with my sister and her husband, Dorine and Vern in Orem.

Our Fisher kids lived in a small apartment in Springville, an easy drive for us to visit for a couple of days before leaving for Holbrooke, Arizona, to meet our son John. It was so good to see him after his being gone for one-and-a-half years. He looked healthy and happy, and anxious to show us around the area. After a meeting with the Mission President and other missionaries, we were off to see the sites. We were privileged to meet several Indian families that John had worked with, becoming quite fond of them, and they of him. In our travels, we also went to a Hopi village high up in the cliffs, meeting with the Elders of the community. They greeted us with respect, and were more than pleased to show us their hogans and relate much history to us. They have totally different traditions and lifestyles from the Navajos as well as just a bit different dialect. The Hopis are also somewhat more reserved and private, we felt very honored to visit with them. From there we drove to Mexican Hat and Monument Valley, stopping along the way for short visits with people that John had taught. Our travels and siteseeing was truly a different experience for Connie and Lisa and me. We then drove to Cameron, Arizona, for a new experience of attending our Sunday meetings with all native speaking people. Of course John understood it all and joined in with them, leaving us speechless, but feeling a wonderful spirit. Our last stop Monday night was at Pinnacle Peak at a nice motel and a huge celebration held outdoors at a well-known restaurant on a hillside. The food and entertainment were superb, and a special treat for me, when John reported to the Master of Ceremonies that it was his dad's birthday. In front of hundreds of people, it was announced for Keith Hancock to stand, and all sing "Happy Birthday" to Keith. It was a total surprise, and certainly a first.

The following day, my actual birthday on the 12th, we drove to Ric and Sheri's home in Sylmar, California, for a several day visit. We took the grandkids to the zoo, and to Sea World, ate at a seafood restaurant, and got very sunburned at the beach, before spending a last day at Magic Mountain going on all of the scariest rides including the very famous monster wooden roller coaster Colossus. While there, we also listened to several band practices of our son's band, Paragon. These practices were held several times weekly in a little studio that Ric built in his garage. Their band performed in many of the well renowned nightclubs both in Hollywood and Los Angeles, such as Chuck Landis, FM Station, Whiskey A Go Go, etc.

After this lengthy visit and experiencing many new and exciting things, it was back to Utah.

We spent several more days visiting with John J, Kris and son J, and some prearranging for John to return to university or college later in the fall. A very busy and full July.

The last half of the year was also very busy experiencing a more than usual number of funerals, many being younger persons. Connie was called upon to sing at quite a number of these funerals as well as several church functions. I was somewhat surprised and amused at how busy our small used appliance business had become. We were going to auctions once or twice a week or following up on private sales, buying appliances to restore and resell in our store. We even came to the point of hiring a man to clean up these units, making them look almost new. Along with this, we were having fun.

The year ended with both businesses doing really well, and kept me hopping to keep up and still be able to spend some time with family whose needs seemed to grow more, as did they.

Whether we are ready for it or not, the New Year does arrive, and what will it bring? More surprises good and bad, prosperous or lean, however it is ours to live and hopefully to enjoy.

Well it did come, early in the spring, almost unexpectedly, but not totally. Although our youngest, Lisa Jill, had been seeing Don Tanner steadily for more than a year, she was still very young and not yet graduated from high school. She informed us that they had decided to get married in May, just a month away. It would seem the saving grace was the fact that Don was in fact seven years older than Lisa, and had been on a mission, and was steadily employed. He worked with his dad on the family corn farm for the better part of the year, and for an oil rig in winter months. Tanner Corn was known far and wide, and harvested and delivered hundreds of tons all over Southern Alberta each year. We also knew his parents, Jim and Hazel Tanner, from their service at the Temple, therefore we felt to bless the marriage rather than object.

As was the case with our first two children, they wanted to hold their reception at our home, which was wonderful, but then added, they would also like the marriage to take place in our home. Unlike our first two, it would not be in the Temple.

This of course was disappointing to Connie and me as well as Jim and Hazel, however, our adult kids make their own decisions, not controlled by parents. Don and Lisa Jill were excited and happy, and the plans went forth. Sometime toward the end of April, Lisa's sister Kristie arrived from Utah to be her maid of honour, and help with other preparations. We expected thirty guests for the wedding, and over sixty showed up. Bishop Morgan Johnson of Barnwell performed the ceremony, and all went as smooth as clockwork. Of course losing my baby girl made me cry as I walked her down the hall to the well decorated and prepared living room where her handsome groom awaited. The young bride looked stunningly gorgeous, with a smile that lit up the entire home. As always our home looked beautiful, filled to capacity with flowers and smiles. The reception held at the church across the street was also filled with several hundred guests with a phenomenal program which included the bride singing several love songs to her groom. Lest I forget to mention, they were sealed in the Temple a few years later before their other three children were born.

Later in that same year, September 1984, my sweetheart Connie and I, were called to serve as officiators in the Cardston Temple, where we remained in that capacity for just over twenty-nine years. At the time of this call, I was at another slump in my business, and felt that I should be putting all of my extra effort into rebuilding, however, without giving it much thought, we said, *yes*, and then wondered how we could handle it. We asked what days or evenings we would be needed. When the answer was, "Well we sure need workers for days." Once again our quick answer was "Okay." What was there to lose? I virtually had little or no business anyway. I was almost frightened to start, but it was not long before we discovered that it was a very fulfilling and rewarding calling, one that we would love for a lifetime.

My poor health has now precluded me from continuing, but during those years we enjoyed many exciting experiences, and acquired many, many close personal friends.

I amusingly calculated that with the number of miles we drove to

Cardston to fill this assignment each week, we would have worn out two cars in the process. In addition to our Temple assignment, we also drove to the town of Foremost for a three year Stake Mission assignment each Sunday. One more fun time for us.

It was a very small branch, however the four main families had a number of young and teenage children, and we really enjoyed teaching classes, and being invited to their farm and ranch homes for special occasions. Once again meeting folks who became very dear friends.

I believe our business to be like most small town communities. We had very slow years and we had really good years. I never had a year that I couldn't pay my secretary her wages, nor slight any of my sales persons, giving them the edge on any listings or sales. At times we had as many as six sales people on staff when things were really moving well. We did have a few nail biting, belt tightening years or times, but always had sufficient to eat, clothes to wear, a car to drive and even take a vacation every year, though at times it may not have been very elaborate.

Our call to serve in the Church branch at Foremost sounded almost a bit more than we could endure, along with our other responsibilities, as it was a full hour drive each way. However, it only took us about twice, when we knew that it was meant to be. We enjoyed all of the families immediately, and they related closely to the two of us. We discovered that all of them also had a long drive, some as much as fifty to sixty miles from their ranch home, usually twice per week. It was a nice little brick building complete with chapel, two small classrooms, an office and a kitchen; the kitchen being well used for lunches and parties. Over our three years of travel, we enjoyed the change of seasons, going from winter to spring when crops were planted, to warm summers and beautiful fall harvests. It was beautiful terrain with lots of grassland as well, teeming with beef cattle, horses and lots of wild life, deer, antelope, moose and elk, along with smaller animals and birds.

Our fieldtrips to their farms and ranches was also a treat never to be forgotten. On one occasion, I was invited to spend three days at the

Ulrich ranch, riding, and rounding up cattle for selling and/or medicating. For them, it was a time of work; for me, it aroused my dreams of the past.

At a future date, the Ulrich brothers, Stan and Dennis, approached me to list and sell this large and beautiful ranch. The two men decided to sell and buy separate ranches. We eventually found a cash buyer, for better than three million dollars; a rancher and trucker who wished to expand his holdings.

It was rather sad for me to see this wonderful property be sold. I had become quite attached to it, however it suited their purposes and certainly gave my business a shot which it needed.

While serving as stake missionaries in Foremost, we experienced many delicious meals, Easter and Christmas parties, sleigh rides and Christmas carolling. Certainly a joyous calling.

The family eventually purchased a beautiful ranch in Manitoba, but we still remain good friends.

One more step forward for a growing family. As a matter of fact, this time we are taking two steps forward, just a little apart; only four days, which would be just two little steps in place of one big one. The mystery here is, two new grandsons, not just one born to our two beautiful vivacious daughters. It was almost a race, and they both won. Dee James Tanner, son to Don and Lisa Jill Tanner, was born September 29th, on Grandpa and Grandma's (Keith and Connie's) wedding anniversary. Devin Hancock Fisher, son of John and Kristie Fisher, born October 3rd, on his father's birthday. What a celebration. DJ, as we called him, had eyes blue as a bright sky, and Dev, as we called him, had eyes the colour of chocolate pudding. They were so different from each other, but both so beautiful. We were so thrilled and proud to be blessed with two more strong healthy boys to grace our family.

Just a few weeks after this exciting event was the call and setting apart of Connie and me as Temple Ordinance Workers to begin our service on September 15th.

Some of the first people that we worked with were three couples approximately twenty years our senior, Maurice and Necia Bennett, Devere and Meg Leavitt and Lindsey and Marie Atwood, all of whom we became close and fast friends with. Over the many years, besides our association with them in the temple, we celebrated all of our birthdays, our wedding anniversaries, picnics and even some vacations together. If there was a special occasion of any sort, the eight of us seemed to get together for it. For some reason, our age differences didn't seem to be an issue. Much of it seemed to stem back to our days of being raised on a farm where we used horses and wagons and worked the land. I seemed to have been raised in a lot of the same era, "the good old days." And now we all drove modern day cars, trucks, large tractors and combines. We also had a TV, electric lights and running water in the house. For me, many of these changes didn't come until I was in my early twenties, not many years after their changes started to come about. We still had many of our former associates, but seemed to have more to talk about and enjoy with these older folks, and always had more fun when we were all together.

On July 30th we were treated with one more beautiful button nose baby granddaughter, Kira Shanelle, also blonde with brown eyes. Thank you, Ric and Sheri. That gave us half as many girls as boys. I like the girls best, but then I was always partial to femininity.

I was once again very busy with listings and sales as well as rentals. One nice thing about the rentals, I had an excellent secretary to handle them, Patricia Anderson. She took right over, not only collecting rents, but repairing minor problems, and shaking up the renters if they tried to skip a month, allowing me more time for the selling end of things.

Connie had been constantly singing at funerals for the last three months; I liked it better when she was barraged with singing at weddings. After spending the summer working in Raymond, our son John returned back to university in Orem, where he graduated with a degree in engineering. The high rate of exchange of $1.40 on our Canadian dollar was making it almost too expensive to send our kids to the States for their schooling, however he did try an unsuccessful semester at the Lethbridge University before becoming disenchanted with it. Meanwhile, John J and Kris moved back to Utah from California so he could finish his schooling at the BYU, where he graduated with a Business Degree. Their two older sons were born in Provo prior to their return to California to live.

Being settled in my own office in Raymond as a full-fledged rural realtor, I was elected to become a director on the Lethbridge Real Estate Board, a position I held for five years. It was by a vote each year of the board members. Our mandate reached south from Claresholm to the Coutts border and west to the Rockies. It was a large area to cover as well as a tremendous responsibility, but we had some great realtors that did a good and thorough job. Each year a Nationwide Real Estate Convention was held in an alternate city somewhere in Canada from east to west. Of course this was always a highlight to meet with other realtors to exchange information on listings as well as a great opportunity to see more of our vast diversified country.

My first and most exciting convention was held in Vancouver, B.C., a beautiful city, very clean and orderly. Between and after meetings, my wife and I walked around the center area of the city to view as many different and exciting places as we could. Downtown Vancouver has many ethnic stores to explore, accommodating the variety of peoples and cultures living in this large city. The sights and smells were so different from our own part of the world, it was like being in a foreign country. Later a tour bus took us around a residential area to see many magnificent homes. We fully enjoyed our tour and walks until time for evening entertainment, awesome programs, dances and the romance of the "Big Bands." Vancouver certainly was more than we had expected.

During the days while the realtors were in meetings, our partners were entertained by trips to museums, an island tour, and luncheons. They were well entertained and well cared for, seeing many interesting things and places. While for me, seeing a man in a trance, walk on a bed of live hot coals, and daring to, and seeing three or four out of the audience accept being put in a trance and then doing the same, was almost too amazing. Over the next several years we enjoyed many conventions with amazing programs, classes and entertainment for both the realtors and their partners.

Out of the many conventions that we attended, one other one comes to mind that was extra special, our first time to Montreal, and our first to be fully immersed in the French language (our *other* Canadian language). Well from the stories that I had been told, I was not that anxious to try to communicate with these foreigners. Happily I was surprised. I not only was treated as a friendly tourist, but as a genuine counterpart, as a fellow Canadian. My first impression of these different Frenchmen, and Women, was very pleasurable, and not at all as I was lead to believe. Most didn't speak English, but tried very hard to be understood and accommodating. I found this to be the case for our complete visit. Mind you, there are always a few idiots in every crowd. The convention was fun and educational, and lots of great entertainment.

When it was over, Connie and I rented a car, touring many places in Montreal, Quebec City, as well as the countryside. We then crossed the border into Vermont, where we viewed the sites of the changing of the leaves, from green to gold, orange, yellow and red. What a glorious sight. The mountains, hills and valleys, came alive with color. The picturesque small communities and farmlands were honed to the smallest detail, what a wonderland. Our return flight was fast and enjoyable, however, we surely would love to travel this vast marvellous land by train at some future date.

For this old farmer/rancher, who didn't especially want to get into the real estate business, I seemed to be having my share of fun and excitement. Connie and I always enjoyed attending our annual real estate banquets, usually held as a year-end Christmas party. One of these more recent parties that we attended with John and Kristie, the Master of Ceremonies announced the name of the Realtor of the Year, by first telling of his or her accomplishments, when I turned to my wife and said, "That person has done some of the same things that I have done," when all of a sudden, the name "Keith Hancock" was announced. I was more than bowled over. I was called up to the stand to receive my award, and after stammering a few words of thanks, I said, "To show how I feel, I want to call my beautiful wife up here to sing *The Impossible Dream*." Of course as a wonderful singer, she obliged, and brought the house down with a standing ovation of more than a thousand people.

During my sojourn as a Director and Vice President, I also had many shorter trips and dozens of meetings as well as adjudicating many problems and complaints whilst also being Ethics Chairman.

When retiring from this position and from real estate, I received a beautiful gift, a nice plaque and a fancy certificate indicating that I was now a "Lifetime Member" of the Real Estate Board.

Although I still can't pass a well-cared for farm or ranch without getting a very nostalgic feeling of wanting to be there, I believe after more than forty-five years as a realtor and several years in the insurance business, I can almost say that this life has treated me and my dear family, well.

Now I must continue on with the next half of my journey, perhaps the better half, including more business adventures, travel, and best of all, my *family!!*

With my son-in-law, John J, starting to take over the reins of the real estate business, I began thinking of getting into an alternate sideline business. Although we had rarely rented a video movie, it sounded somewhat intriguing when the video rental business just through my back lot came up for sale. The price seemed right, and it was close at hand with a couple of excellent clerks to operate it. I talked the matter over with John and Kristie, who informed me that they had also been considering it as a side business. Together we made a decision to purchase it, and to leave it in the strip mall where it now stood. We added several lines of snack goodies along with the video rentals, and felt it to be a fun and profitable business without a lot of extra time and effort. We left it at the same location for the next two years, and then decided to move it to a large building that I owned on Broadway Street which became available. The move was made, and became very successful for many years allowing us to employ a number of young people, including sons of John and Kristie. It remained interesting for several more years and we decided to open a second store in the town of Magrath. We rented a small building on Main Street and went right to work painting inside and out and buying and building the necessary equipment and shelves to also run a successful business.

We were then finding that it was taking more time and effort than we were prepared to take away from our real estate business, and therefore sold the Magrath operation to one of our employees, Dwight Davies. Living in Raymond, he felt that the business was going well enough in Magrath, to also purchase our Raymond Video store, thus leaving us with our real estate business and a small ice cream shop connected to our office building, still keeping us plenty busy.

Family portrait of Al and Ella Hancock with first three children; Dorine, Cal and Keith.

Hancock Dairy Farm South-East of Raymond.

Large Hay and milking barn at Dairy.

Keith age 10 years driving John Deere tractor.

Knight Ranch where horses stabled before
failed trip to Arizona at age 15 years.

Keith's 1951 pick-up truck with Dairy home in background.

Threshing grain on our farm before Mission to Argentina.

Keith's companion with 'well to do' Rancher
and his father in Argentina.

Argentine Rancher (Gaucho) cooking steak on Campos of Argentina.

Keith having Asado Steak (Barbeque) with wealthy Argentine rancher on Campos of Argentina.

Gaucho herding horses on the Argentine campos.

Painting of Gauchos celebrating in front of typical straw and mud thatched house on the campos of Argentina.

Keith and Connie Hancock family: John, Lisa, Ricardo and Kristie.

Keith back to ranching in Alberta, branding calf.

Back lawn of Keith and Connie's home in summer.

Partial front view of our home in summer.

Snow shoveled drive edge to edge with carriage house in background.

Keith wearing same old work hat.

Ted and Keith on Dogsled in North West Territories.

Keith with beard, wearing beaver hat in Yellowknife, NWT.

Honorary Parade Marshall.

Joys and Sorrows

Leading up to this point in our busy lives, we were blessed with several more healthy grandchildren of whom I have not made mention, but with one tragedy. These situations one feels only happen to others but not to yourselves. Just over two years after Kira's birth, Ric and Sheri gave birth to yet one more, sweet healthy daughter, Kandyse Layne Hancock. She was born in Sylmar, California, during a devastating earthquake that literally destroyed the hospital.

Ric had just taken Sheri into the hospital where she was being prepped for delivery, when it struck with a vengeance throwing him to the floor. He was not sure where they had taken his wife, or whether she was injured. As it turned out, she and the baby were safe, but was very frightening for him and others there.

After hearing the story, Connie and I drove to California to be with them and help out with the other children. While there, another more tragic situation took place at home. On Thanksgiving Day, our nephew, Brad Clark, had approached our son John to take our dune buggy out to hills north of town for some hill climbing fun. This they did pulling it behind the truck and taking all precautions for their safety. Brad's friend, Adam Midgely, accompanied them. After a couple of hours up and down the hills, John suggested that they return home, when Brad insisted that they go up the hill one more time only with him on the back seat and John and Adam in the front seats. Half way up the hill, for an unknown reason, the vehicle stalled and began to roll over down the incline. Brad should have been able to jump clear with the other two being injured in the front. Luckily John received only minor injuries, Adam none, however Brad was not so fortunate, and died from injuries shortly after being rushed to the hospital. John, as a returned missionary, gave him a blessing immediately after the accident and felt sure he would be okay, but our Father in Heaven had other plans for Brad, and he did not survive. The loss of Brad's life has remained with our son all of these subsequent years, and has taken a heavy toll on his thoughts and behavior, as well as his health.

That was not the end of this particular episode of our lives. Three months later as we stood near our Christmas tree for family photos of some of our children, the phone rang. It was from California. As well as Ric and Sheri living in California, John J and Kristie lived there; the call was from the Fishers.

"Hello Dad. I am calling to say that Kandyse just died." (Silence), Connie said, "Who died? Kandyse. Kandyse who? (Now crying), our Kandyse." We were both ready to faint with shock and grief, then our children in the room were in the same state. John J. continued to tell us about the sad circumstances. She had died of SIDS, crib death, a known cause of death for hundreds of infants each year. Her daddy, Ric, had played with her that very morning before going to work, Sheri had put the baby in for an afternoon nap, and when later going in to check on her, discovered that she was not breathing, and had already passed away. What a shock for all of them. Paramedics were called; she was rushed to hospital, but was already gone. Our Angel now awaits our joining her. *We love you!*

This being the first death in our growing little family, it was kind of a hard pill to swallow. I realize that many families go through much worse tragedies, and somehow keep their heads up along with their faith, and we can also. It was a great comfort and blessing to our kids to have John and Kristie living just a few miles away, and help take the sting away. Also to help things out, Lisa Jill and our son John drove down with us to Sylmar, thus having all of our family together for the grieving and the funeral.

It was a beautiful service and we all took part in one form or another. The people in their ward and their Bishopric and Relief Society took over all of the arrangements and were a wonderful support. They also had many, many friends who also joined in. When Ric went to pay the expenses he was informed that they had all been taken care of by an anonymous donor. To further care for them, they received many envelopes with cards of sympathy along with more money. The Bishop informed me that "Long after you have returned home, your family will be taken care of." I have never seen a more caring people. Ric and Sheri were truly loved.

The burial plot was under a little tree in a place for children, called "the Land of Nod at Green Haven Memorial Park" in San Fernando Valley. From our own family assistance came a magnificent gesture on the part of John K. when he installed a new engine in Ric's van that had not been operational for some time. He is a fine mechanic, and I told him that I would pay for a new engine if he would install it. When he had completed the job and started the van, it ran and sounded smooth as a kitten.

As most people know, our Church, "The Church of Jesus Christ of Latter-day Saints" (Mormon), is completely run by volunteers, from the President/Prophet right through to the custodians. We are all called to fill some position, some for a short period of time, while others much longer. There is no calling set in stone, nor by money or influence. Any baptised and active person is subject to a call to any position. Women do not bear the priesthood, as is God's call, not man's. As a faithful wife, they jointly bear the blessing of the priesthood with their husbands. To this end, my dear Connie and I have held many positions in the Church, some together, others distinctive and apart. In September of 1984, we were called to serve as Temple Officiators in the Cardston Alberta

Temple, a very humbling and sacred call. It is somewhat time consuming and generally filled by some who are fully retired from work-a-day jobs and/or former church leaders. In our case, just very blessed. We had never been in the habit of turning down any call to serve, and accepted the challenge with much joy, although with much trepidation. I may speak of this calling to some degree later on in my writings, but will conclude now, that for me, it has lasted just over twenty nine years, and Connie 27 years.

Most of our Grandchildren were born during those years, and to us have proven to be the greatest joy of our lives. I am not sure that I will speak of each of them on an individual basis, but can and will honestly say, that I love them all equally, and respect each for their personal talents, schooling, and their accomplishments. I will try to place them in the order of their births, and I do know to whom they were born, and certainly know each as to their gender.

After the untimely loss of our sweet Angel Kandyse, two more husky grandsons were born in that same year. The first of the two was Chase Derek Fisher born to John and Kristie Lee Fisher on July 14^{t,h} just two days after my birthday. He was born in Canada, although his parents still lived in California. The second was Scott Braden Tanner second son of Don and Lisa Jill Tanner born October 20th, while Connie and I were travelling through Washington on our way home from a real estate convention held in Vancouver. It would seem that as much as I love girls, we were destined for mostly boys, but then when they got a little older, I could put them to work in our big yard.

In re-reading a place in my journal, I came to another tragic but happy ending story; involving Ric's family again. Jamin was about seven and on his way home from school with friends, when crossing a well-marked driveway next to the school, a lady came rushing into the drive without looking, striking Jamin with her car, knocking him down and running over his body with the front wheel. His friends began to yell at her, when she put the car in reverse and began to backup. She had dragged him with her front wheel across the asphalt imbedding pavement into his back and arms and would surely have crushed him the second round. Luckily Jamin had enough power and presence of mind to roll out from under the car before becoming unconscious. He was rushed to hospital by ambulance, but as our Father in Heaven would have it, he had no lasting injuries. The trauma still hits him from time to time, but he is alive and well. Another great blessing.

We were determined to have a football team in our family, with two more grandsons born in the next two years. Haydon Ric Tanner arrived on April 9th, to Don and Lisa, making three sons for them, and a fourth son for John and Kristie the following year with the birth of our Presidential grandson on July 4th, Jefferson Monroe Fisher, named for two United States presidents who both succumbed on that same July day. Haydon of course took on the middle name "Ric," after our son Ric, destined to follow in his footsteps as that of a musician, which he ultimately has done.

Listings and sales were going *gang buster* once again, and I was extremely busy. I have noted in my so called "small plates," my daily agenda book, that typically I was either writing up offers or showing two or three properties nearly every day for months on end. One of the more complicated listings that I was attempting to sell was the older large theatre building sitting on our main street. It had long since been occupied as a theatre, and had been renovated years ago to become a hardware store, and Credit Union, which had both failed. Sitting empty for a number of years, it was extremely run down, the roof leaked and had ruined ceilings and more. However, the brick structure was very solid, and the potential for some large business or businesses remained. It had now been taken over by the FBDB, a financial institute, a Government lending department. I showed it to many people for six to eight months, but without success. The government agency just wanted to dump it, and approached me to buy it.

I said "What would I do with it? I already own three commercial properties, and don't need a white elephant on my hands."

They said "Just make us an offer." I told them if they would accept an offer of me paying off just the back taxes owing, I would consider it. I certainly thought they would turn that down, as it was worth many thousands more, however to my surprise, they told me to write up the offer and they would accept it. I did, and they did!

Fortunately we had just sold some oil shares (the few that we had), and had a bit of ready cash. In talking it over with my best friend, my sweetheart wife, she said, "Let's go for it!" And we now owned a huge empty run down building.

The first thing we did was install a new roof, close up some gaps, put in a couple of new doors, paint a little, and start looking for a tenant. To my surprise and delight, there were several who wanted some spaces, but not all. We were able to accommodate them, thus bringing in a few dollars to enable us to do a few more repairs.

Eventually, our high school was about to rebuild the school shop across the alley, and approached us to lease the entire space for a couple of terms. Then an Ammonite business of which our son John was involved with wanted to rent it for their operation for a year or so. Finally a cabinet maker took it over for two more years before leaving some open paint thinner near something flammable that ignited, gutting the back end and part of the roof. As luck would have it, we had good insurance, and the entire building was renovated complete with a brand new four bedroom apartment on the second floor. Once again, a blessing that was unexpected.

Now this building so freshly redone, was a great opportunity for us to move our Video Rental store into this larger space. With very little work, it fit in perfectly with enough room to also move our real estate business into a front area, and with some renovations and some ingenuity on Kristie's part, we also built a cute little Ice-Cream Store in an unused area at the south front side. It was called Tropical Freeze

Ice Cream Parlour and became very popular. It was also very popular with all of our own family; we took advantage of all of the goodies it had to offer. I didn't realize there were so many varieties of ice cream; I think I was required to try them all.

Another girl at last. I love all of our grandsons dearly, but it was sure a wonderful pleasure to know that there were still some more girls in Heaven, and another one was reserved for our family. One more April birthday, Maren Elisa Tanner came to join us on April 2nd. That was no April Fool joke, she was and is, absolutely beautiful and perfect in every way. Born of course to Don and Lisa, in Taber, Alberta, a young sister for three boys, Dee James, Scott Braden and Haydon Ric. I think she is going to be spoiled by her dad and mom as well as by brothers and so many boy cousins, and certainly by Grandma and Grandpa.

Not willing to take a back seat and especially not by a girl, one more grandson came to join in the fun almost exactly a year later. Born April 13th, Jerran Pierce Fisher came to Raymond to complete the family of John J and Kristie Lee, winning the race with now five wonderful healthy handsome sons, enough to form their own basketball team or engage in whatever sport they may choose. If they follow in their dad's footsteps, they will indeed be totally involved in all kinds of sports.

Now in my seventies, it seemed that perhaps it was time for me to slack off a little. I certainly didn't feel that I should retire from business altogether, however, John J and Kristie felt that they would feel more stabilised if they owned their own business rather than employed as to John being a salesperson only. I had given this some thought when they first moved to Canada from California, that some future date I would want John to take over the business in its entirety. Neither of my sons had followed suit in the Real Estate sector, nor had they ever expressed a desire to do so. Ricardo had worked and lived in California since his graduation from University, wanting always to be in the music business, and certainly he was in the right place for that. Our son John Keith had graduated with a degree in engineering and was also living in the United States, with no desire to get into real estate, but to do his own thing in whatever else struck his fancy. Don Tanner was a farmer through and through, and since John J had become acquainted with real estate in Utah and seemed to find his niche in this hectic business, he seemed to be the logical one to eventually take it over. The deal for their purchase was made and they were now the owners of Coldwell Banker Hancock Land Corp.

With me now becoming a salesperson for John, I had been the owner of a number of businesses since my early twenties, and should have been quite content to sit back with someone else having the worries and responsibility. However, when it is one of your own family, a person still feels every move whether it is good or bad. In my case, after more than fifty years of being the boss or overseer of many businesses, I went into a state of depression, flopping on my bed and crying for days on end. I think I hid that from family pretty well as I fought with myself to maintain my sanity. I am not sure when I finally overcame the down feelings, but know that the urge to be in my own business, or be running a farm, still hits me occasionally even after these many years.

Keith's Corner

FORTUNATELY I FOUND A FEW CAUSES TO TAKE ON ALONG WITH still selling a few properties. The one I fought the hardest for and am somewhat proud of came in 1999. A new four-lane highway # 4, had recently been completed from the Canada/US Border at Coutts, Alberta, and running to the city of Calgary and on. It is located nine miles north of our community and is used extensively by our citizens and others. I had sold a home in Raymond to a couple from northern Alberta, who whilst moving here, crossed this highway at night with a load of furniture. Sadly enough, they did not see an unlit semi-unit truck on the darkened intersection, driving into the side of it, and the lady was killed. This brought the total to eight people that I personally knew who had been killed there in the space of six years. Overhead highway lights had not been installed on this major intersection, and when inquiring about this to government officials, I received an answer back from them, that a study had been done, and lights were not necessary at that particular intersection.

Being the hardheaded person that I am, I did not take *NO,* for an answer. I immediately contacted our Town council and other nearby communities about this, and was informed by all, that they had also tried, and that they would not be put in place there. My answer was *"We'll see!"* I have never been one to give up easily, and this became a challenge to me.

I began writing letters along with some phone calls. Each letter that I wrote to our MLA, or Transportation Minister, or Premier, I sent a copy to the nearby TV and radio stations, the newspapers, mayors of towns, president of A.M.A for the Province, Chambers of Commerce and anyone else that I thought might have some clout. Along with the letters, I sent drawn diagrams and photos of this busy spot. By so doing, my letters couldn't be ignored nor thrown in the trash. After nearly one-and-a-half years and dozens of letters back and forth, some very strong, I received a letter from the Minister stating, that fourteen lights would be installed. Along with this request for lighting, I also petitioned for shoulders to be added from that intersection, running to the Town of Raymond, another badly needed safety measure. When the T.V. station came to interview me at the site, the young lady said, "Now where is the other intersection you stated also need to be lit?" I said "Let's get in your car and drive down the highway and I will point it out to you." We drove south several miles, when she said, "Now where is it?"

I said "We have already passed it, turn and go back." She had missed it completely as it was not well marked. After more camera shots and interview, she remarked that it surely did need lights there as well. We now have them installed. The newspapers had me in their headlines, "Man Wins Battle, but Not the War." The Wilson Corner is now called *Keith's Corner* by many people. Many that I don't know have thanked me for my efforts. Since that time, I was also able to get the Transportation Minister to install three more sets of highway lights at intersections turning into Barnwell, Alberta, where some of my children lived.

It is rather a good feeling to know that you have achieved something that took some personal effort.

To go along with this story, the following year our community awarded me with the honour of *Citizen of the Year*. I accepted this with great humility. What I had achieved surely would have been done by someone at some future date. Thank you Raymond, you are *my* town.

The Golden Years

My brother-in-law, Ted Lybbert, Connie's sister's husband, and I had become good buddies over the years and enjoyed doing things and going places together. One of our common things was to go fishing on one of the mountain streams nearby, or at Police Lake, usually with our canoes. On occasion Connie and Carole would accompany us with a picnic lunch. I was never sure enough of myself to catch a fish for lunch or supper, so a nice meal was always prepared ahead of time. As Ted was a high school teacher, he enjoyed summers relaxing on these short jaunts. Ted had built a beautiful wood slat canoe in his spare time to travel along with my pretty yellow fibreglass lake canoe that I had purchased. My skills at canoe building or any type of building was not my forte, so finding this yellow beauty which I named "Maren," after a pretty girl, our granddaughter, made for some fun trips to the mountains.

On one such trip, we drove to Cameron Lake at Waterton Park where we could, and had in the past, paddle to the far end of the ice-cold lake, and get out to walk on a glacier. It was a long paddle, but fun and always interesting. We had been on the smooth lake for about one half hour enjoying the bright blue summer sky and the rugged snow-capped mountains when a terrific wind came up, bringing snow and hail with it. We felt we should head for shore when the waves got huge and overwhelming. Ted had already let Carole out on the shore and had gone on. I started to paddle hard and turn the canoe toward shore when Connie panicked and paddled against me, saying "What is going to happen to us? We will drown."

The canoe was struck hard on the side by a big wave and we tipped over, filling our boat with water. I managed to upright it once, but over again it went. I yelled through the storm to Connie, to just hang on to the front and I would get us over to the shore. I then went under the canoe where there was air space, and dog paddled toward shore. When Connie's feet hit ground, she looked back, couldn't see me and thought I had drowned. Luckily I was exhausted but okay. The icy water had brought Connie into a state of hypothermia for a short time and other than being wet and very cold we were still alive and okay. Two weeks later, two men died of hypothermia at the lake under similar circumstances. One more great blessing to our credit.

That same fall, Ted decided to retire from teaching in the Raymond school and head for greener pastures, or I should really say, for whiter pastures. He took a position of teaching at Hay River in the North West Territories at almost double the salary. At Christmas time, he returned home for a month, and then had one more month of teaching. They had very short school terms for the native children. Before returning, he approached me to return to the Territories with him for that extra month. My answer was "What on earth would an active real estate man do up there for a month?"

He said, "You're semi-retired, it is winter, what could be more fun?" Well I had always had a desire to travel north, so why not! Connie encouraged me to go, and it didn't take long for me to pack a few things along with a sleeping bag, sheet of foam on which to sleep, and my camera, and off we went. I was many months behind on writing my journal, and decided that would keep me busy for the next month getting caught up, along with a whole lot of sightseeing. When I returned I felt that I should write an article or short story about my experience in the North, and would like to insert that experience and/or story, in this writing at this point. If I try to duplicate it here and now, I may forget some important happenings.

North of Sixty

THIS ARTICLE WAS PUBLISHED IN THREE SEGMENTS OF THE LOCAL newspaper Raymond Expressions, and was very well received, with many people saying, "I can hardly wait to read the next issue."

The sky was clear and brilliant with millions of stars; the air was cold and crisp when we arrived at the northern-most border sign of our Province of Alberta.

My brother-in-law, Ted Lybbert, had made this journey many times in the past two years, but I was a novice. The thrill of travelling to the North West Territories (north of the Sixtieth Parallel) had never been a consideration for me, however, it was now happening. I said when I first saw the sign "Stop the car Ted. I want to get out." Well he did, and I jogged the one hundred yards or so across the line into the *true north,* the **North West Territories,** standing strong and free. I cannot sufficiently express the exhilarating feeling that came to me on that cold night.

This was to be the beginning of an exciting thirty-day adventure for me. Ted had taught school for the past two years at the Hay River Diamond Jenness High School, and had just one more month before taking retirement.

After the Christmas holidays, he invited me to accompany him to the town of Hay River (approx. 4000 people) to spend that last month. What on earth would an active realtor do for a whole month in such an out of the way, out of our world, place??

I soon found the answer!! It was *not* as out of the way as I had thought, and it was *not* as out of our world as I had imagined. As a matter of fact, I met many quite ordinary people who live and work there, and believe it or not, they aren't even of the Eskimo(Inuit) variety. Some of the first people that I ran into were our very own Brian and Dianne Dudley, who had been there for nearly three years, and who were also teaching in a Hay River school.

What do you know, with warm clothes, and sporting a first time ever brand new "beard", I survived the cold, and was in fact, quite comfortable. For most of the time, the daytime highs ranged from minus 20c to minus 34c, with minus 40 to 44c at night. We did feel a chilling minus 62c wind chill on a few but rare occasions.

Most of my daytime activity was writing and catching up on my long delayed journal, over four years of almost forgotten years and going to the public library, reading, and going for long walks on a beautiful wooded trail along side of the frozen-over Hay River adjacent to the town site.

Our fourth night there, at 1:00 AM, the phone rang. It was Dianne. "Do you want to see the Northern Lights?" I couldn't wait for this experience. It was chilly to say the least, going from a warm sleeping bag to a cold car to drive to the edge of town for a better view; but worth it? I'll say it was!

I never experienced anything quite like it. Of course I have seen the great Aurora Borealis on many occasions as it is present in our part of the world, but nothing like the rivers of light that we saw in that great country. For the most part they appeared in a greenish shade, jumping streaking, twirling as they gyrated across the northern skies, a truly magnificent sight to behold for as many hours after dark as you would care to watch. Even to this date, they remain a mystery for the most part, conjuring up many legends with the native peoples and keeping scientists scratching their heads for a correct answer.

Another wonderful experience was a trip to Yellowknife, the Capital of the N. W. T. We left Hay River at about 5:00 A.M. in the morning, to Fort Providence where we crossed the mighty McKenzie River on an ice-breaking ferry boat. It would cease running for the winter soon as the ice becomes too thick to break up, at which time an "Ice Bridge" would be used to cross the Great Slave Lake.

Our trip to Yellowknife was an arctic journey of the most beautiful winter scenery in the world. There were trees and underbrush so thickly covered with frost and snow that the word "white" pales by comparison. I took many pictures and videos, but they don't begin to bring out the sheer beauty of this wondrous sight. The city of Yellowknife was extremely interesting, and boasted of all the amenities that each of us enjoy, complete with large hospital and even Canadian Tire and Dairy Queen. The part of the city they call "Old Town" was of most interest to us with quaint restaurants, shops and pontoon equipped airplanes by the score. Most everyone drives snow mobiles around the streets along with automobiles, so when you fill at a gas station, you must wait in line with these powerful machines, for a tank of gas.

Our return trip was uneventful, however we did take occasion to side trip into three different native villages for interest sake, once again competing for the road with large fancy snow machines.

The town of Hay River has lots of things to keep one occupied summer and winter, but one of the things that I enjoyed the most was a large waterfall several miles to the south, called Alexandra Falls on the Hay River.

In the winter with most of the water frozen over, there is an area of open water where it flows over the rocks into a gorge about 200 feet down. The open water causes steam to rise up bringing about a huge dome of snow and ice making it into a volcano-like area. Humongous icicles of many colors form along cliffs nearby making it quite an attraction at this time of the year.

Perhaps the greatest experience and thrill of my life came toward the end of my stay with the opportunity to travel on a real dogsled with a real live dog team. I shall treasure this dream forever more.

Both Ted and Brian have helped with the care of sled dogs belonging to the owner of these dogs, Danny Beck, for the past two years, and have become quite proficient in the handling of the several teams of dogs from Danny's kennel. I stated emphatically that I wasn't returning home until I also went for a run.

It was very cold the day that we went, but every moment was a joy. Hooking up the teams is an experience in and of itself to behold: dogs barking so loudly and running and jumping on their individual doghouses and tugging at their leashes so anxious to be chosen for the run. Harnessing and hitching to the sled is like trying to hold back ten race horses champing at the starting gate. Then off we go on a trail of indescribable beauty, a creek bottom in summer, a dog sled trail in winter, with snow and thickly frost covered trees and brush, where for the most part, only animals traverse.

We see huge tracks made by wolves and get a quick glimpse of one watching from a distance. Ravens and rabbits by the score further bring us to the wilds of nature. We turn toward the frozen Great Slave Lake with its jagged hills of ice and snow. The ten dogs run in complete unison, each pulling his or her equal share at a speed of approximately 18 to 20 miles per hour. Small chunks of ice from their paws flip up and hit you in the face, which of course is already frozen from the wind chill; but these powerful dogs don't tire or slow down. "How long can they run like this?" I asked.

"Oh, if they are in really top shape, 30 to 50 miles without stopping!" was the answer.

Wow, was I impressed. I travelled about ten miles through out of this world scenery, and with the sun setting, and shining through the trees, glistening on the snow like streaks of gold, my dream ride was complete.

A trip to the Frozen North you say? It is a prominent and vital part of *our* great country of Canada and I am proud that it is. If you ever have the privilege and opportunity to spend some time in the North, buy yourself a big furry beaver hat as I did, grow a beard, white or black, or both, as I did, and do it. You will never regret it; nor will your wife, you men. In fact my wife openly cried when I shaved off the beard!

Thoughts and Back Roads

As told in my story of the *Cold North*, I had a very enjoyable visit, or vacation in a place that I had never been, but perhaps had only dreamed of doing. To get back to some realities of life, the world is filled with tragedies, many of which is difficult to understand. As in many cases, some of the worst disasters hit the poorest nations and people. In reading back to some earlier times, I see where a huge earthquake hit Mexico City, probably the highest populated city in the world, with over eighteen million people. In many of these huge metropolises, the slum areas are wall-to-wall shacks and people. At the particular date that caught my attention, over six thousand had lost their lives, and more to come. Of course there were tens of thousands injured and left homeless, with cost of the damage to the city in the billions. The world at large has come to the aid and support of the people of Mexico, and many stories told of heroic and touching rescues. No matter how many problems we ourselves find, there are much worse circumstances around us, and that there is a power so much greater than us who is in control of all things. All can be well for us one minute and our whole world can topple in the next.

About this same time, a provincial election was called with a nominating meeting to be held in the town of Magrath. I had become somewhat interested in the political arena and particularly anxious to have a good person representing our area. There were four good men running for the nomination, and I believe any one of them would do a pretty good job for us, however one seemed to be a little more qualified in my opinion, therefore I felt we should attend the meeting. Much to my surprise and delight, the school gym where it was to be held was filled to capacity and overflowing. More than twenty five hundred delegates swarmed the floor, far more than there was seating. To me, it was a wonderful sight to think so many cared. It was somewhat reminiscent of my try at politics. In any event, the person that won the nomination was Jack Ady for the Conservative party, and the man that we felt would be the most qualified. There was a lot of hoopla, and we didn't arrive home for bed until 2:30 in the morning, and were up again before five A.M. to get ready for our day of serving at the Temple. I had worked with Brother Gilbert Smith that day, who seemed perfectly well, however, within two more days, he passed away of a heart condition. One never knows how soon they may be taken, and we should all realistically be ready for such an event.

A beautiful event that took place was an Adult Dinner Dance held in Taber, along with a marvellous program after the superb meal. The theme of the evening was music from Broadway Musical Hits. Every number performed was excellent with wonderful props and costuming, and of course for this very proud mom and dad was our Lisa Jill's performance. We have been thrilled to hear her sing many times but have never witnessed her doing any choreography with her singing, so this was a first for us as well as for her. Lisa only had one week's notice to prepare, but appeared as though she had had a lifetime of experience. She sang "I Could Have Danced All Night," from the musical "My Fair Lady." She came on stage wearing a beautiful long nightgown and flowing peignoir, as a prop. There was a large four-poster bed which she danced around as she sang. She literally floated as she sang and danced, it was breathtaking and brought tears to my eyes and joy in my heart. She was so beautiful; it was like watching a gorgeous movie star with angelic qualities. The audience of some six hundred were also awestruck. The organizers afterwards said "We heard you could sing but had no idea that you had that kind of talent. This is just the beginning for you." Well of course the important thing is that she accepted the assignment at the last minute, and was willing to share her God given talents to bring joy to so many people.

    Early in the spring, we experienced some extra warm weather along with warm winds that quickly melted the ice covered rivers in the Cardston area, causing huge chunks of ice to break away from each other, floating down stream, flooding banks, crushing corrals, fences, buildings, trees and animals, many of which were marooned on islands or simply drowned under the monstrous ice flows. Hundreds of cattle were brought to their deaths. Our friend Maurice Bennett lost twenty-seven head of his best beef cattle. This disaster took place in less than one half hour. The entire area looked like a rock avalanche had thundered down a mountain over the many miles. Oh the mighty power and wrath of nature! Mankind is so insignificant compared to our God. I can only expound on the great blessings that we enjoy in this corner of the earth. For the most part, this is the safest part of the world, a little area that few people know about. *Let's keep it this way!!* Many years ago, and more particularly since several of our own family have moved to the United States, and moreover, two of our children and kids, have moved to sunny California to make their permanent homes, I have wondered why anyone would want to live in cold ol' Canada! Well I have over time decided that it isn't such a bad idea. We don't get to live near the ocean, which I dearly love with ocean blue water and the soft white sand. Near the area where we usually stop to have our picnic lunch and wade in the cool water finding sand crabs or building sand castles, there is a fun Fish and Chip café. Their food is always to perfection, and to breathe in the salt air is to die for. At times such as that, I wonder why my ancestors didn't discover California instead of the cold wretched old prairies. Then I search my mind for an answer, and remember having some days like this day that I am sitting in my air conditioned office, writing a story. The day is 34 degrees Celsius (in the 90s), the sky is perfectly clear and there is not even a breeze. Who needs that kind of treatment everyday of their lives? As well as this day, the crops and gardens in the area are phenomenal this year. The peace and freedoms and plenty that we are experiencing so far this season are a grand wonder. Unfortunately, or perhaps *fortunately*, this situation doesn't always happen here, mostly we have to worry a lot, pray a lot, and work damn hard. It does bring a lot of humility. And as I said in a previous statement, "Let's keep it this way." Our grandparents obviously knew what they were doing.

Certainly our lives are truly tested, and sometimes more of a heartbreak rather than just a temporary test, I told of the beautiful crops, this was a July/August day, we had not yet reached September, the big harvest month. The rains started early in the month, not a bad thing in of itself, then stopped. Hooray, the combines were ready and raring to get started, the rains came again, well things can hold off for a while longer. It stopped again, the fields began to dry, not quite enough when the rain began in earnest. The grain fields began to be soggy, they wouldn't hold harvesting equipment, and the grain was soft and sopping wet. Many farmers, both grain, beets and corn were losing all. They had counted on this perfect yield so heavily that many had gone far into debt for extra land, machinery and seed. Where oh where are the sunny beaches of California and Hawaii? Believe me, it all sounds nice, but they are not without their own problems.

A couple of years ago, the Canadian Government came out with a new "Young Farmers" program, to lend these young people money at a low rate of interest, that they might take over their family farms. Theoretically it sounded good, but with two or three bad years in a row, it simply meant that the Farm Credit Corp. began taking over the farms that were delinquent. As a realtor in this area, one day I received a list of 234 farms that had been foreclosed on and were now for sale by this Corporation. My list was for me as a realtor to sell them at cheap prices. When I viewed the numbers, many that I personally knew, it nearly made me cry. Even half of my brother's farm was listed, which he had sold to his son, Bruce. My brother Cal, attempted to buy it back by way of secret bidding, but was unfortunately outbid by a neighbor by a very small margin. The farm had been in our family for four generations. Some of the crops were eventually gathered in very late in the fall, but produced poor grades and yields. Most of the beet and corn crops were saved.

As forever, we have enjoyed, bumper crops, poor crops, medium quality crops, and many scary on the edge crops. Like the saying of a box of chocolates, when all is said and done, you never know what you are going to get! The land can look healthy, the moisture just right for planting, weeds are undercontrol, the crops grow tall full and straight, and then about half way through July, a strong wind arrives with a disastrous hail storm that wipes the fields clean. This year our area had hail the size of golf balls hit, breaking holes through our fibreglass solarium. Luckily our garden was saved as were most of the surrounding crops.

Two years ago, the Town of Cardston took a beating from the hail that measured the size of baseballs, breaking hundreds of windows, including some skylights at the Temple, totalling out nearly every residential roof in town, and putting hundreds of large dents in every car that was in the open. The grain crops and gardens were completely annihilated for miles around. Thank our Heavenly Father that this only happens to this extent, once in many years.

The insurance companies were on the hook for millions of dollars. However, as a former adjuster and claims manager for a large insurance company, I know for a fact that in the interim, they make millions of dollars, and can well afford this setback on occasions. Because of these heavy claims, we have all been severely punished by heavy premiums and huge deductibles.

It certainly is not my intention to get into the disasters of the day, if this were the case, I would not have room to write my own life problems and joys, and after all, that is my main objective and concerns. However, to bring to remembrance the reality of life, I must insert some of the more stark happenings if and when they come to mind, which simply means, they may not always be in sequence of their taking place.

One of many great disasters that struck our beloved United States was totally unexpected nor even predicted and is frighteningly known by the world at large as "9/11."

Over time there have been situations take place that have brought about more deaths in one swelled sweep, or many more millions of dollars in property loss, but this catastrophe involved a terrorist invasion on our sacred soil. On a bright clear morning in September, four huge jet liners were hijacked all at the same time and place, and then commenced their destructive paths, two over New York City, one over Washington DC, and the fourth over Pennsylvania (final destination unknown).

The first two flew into the twin 110 Story World Trade Towers, striking about the 85th floors. Carrying more than ten thousand gallons of jet fuel, the results were predictable. Fires immediately erupted, and minutes later one building after the other plunged to the ground, swallowing up all who were inside, and many passersby. The third jet plane minutes later struck the Pentagon Building in Washington DC, while the fourth (conflicting with passengers) crashed into a farm field in Pennsylvania, killing all aboard. The final count as near as can be estimated, killed over three thousand people, including 343 firefighters and/or police personnel; a heavy toll on innocent lives. Intense investigation showed the terrorists to be Islam's of the al Qaeda group, lead by Osama bin Laden.

While I am on a bit of a sour theme, I will mention another world disaster, and then back to much more pleasant memories. It may because of my age that I am noticing more horrific storms of life, I hope that may be the case however, most scientific evidence would differ, it seems that as the earth also ages, so do the natural disasters come about, and that does not account for the many tragic wars and conflicts between peoples and countries. I must have been in a dream world, or had my head in the clouds, or in a pile of manure. I had not until the monstrous tsunami of December 26th even remembered hearing that term. It was shown on our colour TV right while it was still in progress. I had never in my lifetime seen anything that remotely equalled that kind of destruction. People, mostly tourists, were leisurely on the beaches in Thailand and other small islands, soaking up the sun, surf boarding, boating and swimming, when huge waves were spotted heading to shore, some stood paralysed in their tracks, others scurried to shore, those on shore hurried into the hotels, but all for *not*, the waves came as tall as the hotels, the destruction of buildings, trees and boats came The loss of lives in the tens of thousands, as were the beaches and other property washed clean as the virgin sands while wave after wave crashed into the land. Nothing was left standing except those who managed to reach the highest of ground above the angry waves. Screams of terror were heard as the few that were left searched frantically for any family that may have escaped. Very few miracles occurred, but for a handful of people; some did indeed find their loved ones. Later on the broadcast, several other areas were shown, some small islands were totally washed over with no known survivors.

    I have always had a fear of earthquakes and tornados, however, after seeing this tsunami take place worlds away, and after my small experience with the power of the ocean while in Brazil, I have gained a whole new respect for oceans, rivers, lakes, and just plain water.

    I must render the above thoughts with a little tongue in cheek, as I have always teased my wife a little about her fear of water. In actuality, we were presented with an opportunity soon after this, to go on an Alaskan cruise with some good friends. Connie had balked because of her fear of water, and of course I was raring to go, not fearing anything. I must now eat crow and apologise for my overzealous attitude, but I still want to go, and hope we will all be taken care of, or at least all of us meet our Maker at the same time. I just hope my story will be good enough??

As a few pages back telling of my personal experience in the North, I would once again like to indulge in publishing our account, as written by me at the time, of our cruise to Alaska.

North By Northwest

ALASKA? SOUNDED AWFULLY COLD TO THIS OLD SENIOR CITIZEN, but then I quickly remembered my thirty days in the North West Territories just a few short years ago during the cold month of January. The short days, the long walks on the icy shores of the Great Slave Lake, the dogsled rides and the amazingly beautiful light show displayed by the Aurora Borealis as it gyrated and danced across the chilled nighttime northern skies. All wondrous to me and a thrill of a lifetime to spend time "North of Sixty."

Now we were being approached by our very good friends, Floyd and Rula Smith to join them on a cruise to Alaska. My immediate reaction was, "Sure, why not, it sounds fun." Connie's more swift and positive vocal thoughts were, "No, forget that dumb idea." Her experience on water in the past was not always good, and she wasn't about to get out on a ship, boat or canoe for any reason. Well in spite of her strong objection, I doggedly went ahead with plans to go, and on June 7th we were on a plane to Vancouver, heading for the cruise ship Norwegian Sun, for the trip of a lifetime.

We both enjoy flying, so this was no problem, and we have been to Vancouver two or three times in the past, so that was enjoyable, but my Connie still had some trepidation about embarking on a ship to take her on the water. "The water is so deep and wet, and what if the ship sinks?" Well as it turned out, there was about forty fellow Temple Officiators on this cruise, several of whom were very close friends, and at least that many other people that we knew from around our area. Dr. Bob Russell from our Tuesday shift said," It won't sink, if anything happens, it will go straight up."

By this time she was resigning herself to the cruise, and by second day, she was loving it just like the rest of us. One of the more enjoyable things was the food; eat all you want and when you want, and what you want. The other special treat was the fabulous entertainment of almost any kind that suited your fancy, found in every part of the ship. At night there were theater performances on the big stage that thrilled us to the utmost, and performed by some of the greatest stars in their field. It seemed that we were running from one delightful experience to the next. The weather was to perfection, sunny but not too hot, with blue skies for the most part. Our particular ship held 2200 passengers and approximately 1000 crewmembers to look after your every need.

Our first stop was at Ketchekan, Alaska, seemingly a sleepy little town on the seacoast. However, as with every stop at these communities, several thousand tourists from four or five cruise ships disembarked for a day of shopping and sightseeing every day of the week. The stores were shoulder to shoulder with people and of course "must have" bargains at every turn. We have a house full of souvenirs, so we were not really enticed with shopping, but it was fun to look.

Back to the ship for more good food and entertainment, and sailing throughout the night. That first night, the ride was just a bit bumpy as we crossed currents that were close to shore, but it was short lived, and by mid-morning the ocean had smoothed out to a quiet Cadillac ride, warm and sunny.

There always seemed to be plenty of things to do, we could eat, and then eat, and then eat some more. Actually there were things to keep us occupied such as art exhibits and auctions, lectures pertaining to Alaska, gymnastic areas etc. or one could simply relax in the sun on deck chairs, or even swim in one of the two beautiful pools or lounge in one of the five hot spas on deck. And then eat again.

Our third day out, June 13th, after a night of travel, we pulled into port once again at Juneau for a quick trip into town for a couple of hours, and then back aboard ship for a leisurely trip to see the floating icebergs and up the Fjord as far as we could travel to view the "Sawyer" Glacier. What a wonderful sight this was. We sailed between the great walls and streaked cliffs where the glaciers had been many, many years previous, while smashing through small icebergs as we made our way through to the glacier. One of the more phenomenal sights were the smaller icebergs that gave off the most beautiful blue hue that eye could behold or lips could tell.

When reaching our destination, the ship made a U- turn to take us back to our previous route. The passage was so narrow, that we barely had space to turn. A small craft was sent out into the waters to guide the turn-around. What fun this was, and what a thrill to behold.

Back to one more night of sailing throughout the night. The evening started with our group of eight, (all of us close friends) dining in a plush restaurant. I ordered the best of steaks each night with all of the trimmings, while others dined on succulent seafood etc. Filled to capacity, we made our way to the big stage for quite another feast of entertainment, so varied that it is difficult to describe in few words, but needless to say, the best money could buy if you attended in New York, Las Vegas or Branson.

Not having enough of that, we then sat in the various lounge areas until midnight each night to be entertained further by a marvelous Philippine combo, and other areas of delightful talents. We couldn't seem to get enough. They were all superb. Morning of the 14[th,] a Thursday, we landed in the town of Skagway to spend the day.

We started with our usual hearty breakfast before leaving the ship, and made our way to shore, first having a look in the many shops and stores, and then arranged for a bus tour of the town site and subsequently an exciting trip to the White Pass summit where we ultimately arrived in the Yukon within the borders of Canada. Our driver was entertaining and very knowledgeable of the area.

We stopped a number of times both directions where we could get off the bus to take pictures, view the gorgeous scenery, the magnificent waterfalls, and hear stories of the old Gold Rush days.

I have always felt that Banff and Jasper were the ultimate in mountain scenery, but this was the most picturesque place I have ever seen for stark raw beauty.

At the summit we walked on the glacial-like snow, enjoyed all of the small lakes and wild flowers. Once again a thrill of a lifetime.

Another fun filled evening on board the ship of dining in a fancy restaurant, to the theater for a magnificent program and then on to the various lounges for more entertaining music and snacks. Our room steward left an animal of some sort on our bed, made from uniquely folded towels, and a delicious chocolate on each pillow every night. Just one more fun thing.

Again we traveled throughout the night, however, I should mention that early evening we were fortunate to see a couple of whales following the ship, leaping from the sea to surface and then back. Friday morning after breakfast, Connie went to the beauty salon for a new hairdo while I sat in a hot tub and lounged in the sun on the deck and visited with friends. Later we lunched and looked around the ship. As usual we had a great meal with friends and another fantastic show at the main theater. This also was a special night on the ship as they put on a Chocolate Feast. Everything was made with chocolate, dozens of cakes, truffles, squares, brownies, dipped fruit etc. and animals made from chocolate. All looked great and tasted even better.

Saturday 16th was to be our last full day and evening. I tried to eat enough to last several days, but that didn't work so well, you can only stuff so much in. It was an extremely special evening in any event.

On the big stage in the main theater was to be a talent night for any of the guests who cared to perform. There were about twelve numbers of different varieties from solos to comedy routines. My sweetheart Connie, was persuaded by myself and the dozens on board who knew and loved her singing, to enter the contest. She looked gorgeous, and sang her heart out; singing "The Impossible Dream," the more than a thousand people that packed the theater gave her cheers, whistles, and a standing ovation. It was wonderful.

The ship organizers were looking for a younger person that they could hire on permanently so called the winner to be a young man who had much yet to learn, but did a pretty good job. I was so very, very proud of you my darling as were our numerous friends. My Connie and I ate at our favorite restaurant after the performance, and enjoyed each other's company talking and watching the darkening sky with the moon sparkling across the waves. All in all, we enjoyed this our first cruise so very much and are sufficiently enchanted to sign up for another Cruise in our future. I know that my beauty is quite in agreement with this plan and has at last gained her "sea legs" and has at long last mastered her fear of water. Well at least on *big* water.

More Thoughts and Back Roads

As I approach a bit closer to retirement age, and at this point, I am not sure what that age is, it would seem that I have less to report. Many of my days are kicking back a little more on the work end, and perhaps approaching more of an advisory capacity. Not that all of my advice is taken, or maybe not even wanted. I am still a licenced realtor, however, it would seem that more and more folks that stop in looking for a home to buy, are asking for John or one of the other sales people. In those cases, it makes me feel more of a sore thumb than a useful realtor. I am still enjoying coming into the office, attending meetings, and growling over things that I have no control over. My father was a good mayor of our community for many years, responsible in large part for bringing natural gas into town, getting Main Street paved as well as other streets, and many other useful and needed facilities. I sometimes wonder if I should follow in his footsteps and throw my hat into the arena, but then I look at some of the other things that I have achieved for our town and the area at large, and feel that I should back off, and let "George" do it. If I do that, then I really should not complain about anything! For several years, I have served on many committees, and at present sit on the board of the Historic Society, hoping to preserve a part of the past. I do believe that through my efforts and that of my friend Alan Heggie, we did manage to keep our stampede grounds intact. It was slated to be removed two or three miles east of town, onto an off the road site, not rebuilding the Grandstand or the many other buildings. This would have been heart breaking and a huge mistake. Raymond is known as the "Home of the First Stampede" in Canada, and existed twelve years before Calgary, a now world famous *Out Door Show*. Raymond Knight, a well-known rancher in his day, was largely instrumental in the start-up of the Calgary Stampede in 1912. His livestock and cowboys were the basis of the show in Calgary, twelve years after Raymond put on the first of its kind.

Even this many years later, I still remember the wooden sidewalks that graced the main commercial street in front of the stores and cafes. I well remember the freshly made bread that came out of Alvin Jones' ovens, just a short walk on our ice skates from the outdoor ice rink, to buy for 8 or 10 cents a loaf of scrumptious un-sliced bread to rip apart and share with friends. I remember vividly the owner of Fat's Cafe, a well-rounded short Chinaman, who always waved a butcher knife at us and threatened to box us up and send us to China if we got too smart-mouthed. And then there was John Horvath, the shoemaker, whose shop always had a strong smell of leather and oil; he could repair anything as good as new from a harness to a fine pair of cowboy boots. They are nostalgic days. Our young gang, usually four of us got a kick out of buying one bottle of pop with four straws, and then pay for it with a ten dollar bill that one of us fortunately had at the time. The bottle of pop was 6 cents.

While reminiscing, I am reminded of a short story that I wrote a few years ago with regard to an old chair that sat outside for many years, I called it: *The Old Wooden Lawn Chair*.

"From my bedroom window each night as I kneel in prayer, I gaze out into the moonlight shadows before and after my prayer, and view the old wooden lawn chair. It has occupied this position for many years through the scorching blaze of the sun in summer, the sometimes torrential rains of spring, the falling leaves of a gentle autumn and the harsh blizzards of winter. It has not been removed from its location since being placed out of the way, having given up the ghost of usefulness so many years ago. Often in my mind as my prayers ascend heavenward, I think about the old chair, wondering if it will be there when my work is done on earth, when I have fulfilled my usefulness to family and mankind. I am not yet old by today's standards, however I have reached the stage in life of retirement from a "job well done" so to speak, with some time on my hands to sit back and contemplate what does lie in the future. My health remains pretty good for some things, but is waning in others. I continue to serve in the Temple of our Lord which I have done with my beautiful wife, my eternal companion, for nearly 26 years, and take occasion to visit with a few of our aged and infirm friends on a near weekly basis, watching many of them fade away to their wonderful reward. But what about me? What about that old chair that has passed it's time, yet lives on in memory? Life can be short with much happiness, but can also be fraught with tears and the harshness of living, sometimes as though being seared by that scorching sun or enduring the blast of an icy winter. Ah, but alas, we do have the continued presence of a Heavenly Being, the sweet peace and comfort of the Holy Spirit, and the warmth of a loving companion and family to shield us from being tossed into the outer extremities of our usefulness; like the *old wood lawn chair."*

Throughout our married lives we have taken many nice vacation trips as well as the many business trips to a variety of places. I have told of a few of these trips as I remember them, as well as actually getting a few of them in the correct sequence. It was never my intention to follow an otherwise interesting life, with exact details and dates, mostly it has been as things came to mind. I am not apologising for this shortfall, but somewhat excusing some confusion of dates and happenings.

One of our many vacation trips to California to visit Ric and Sheri and kids turned out much more than we or anyone had expected. As was taking place by far too many times in those years, four white policemen took opportunity to pull a black man over, who obviously had been drinking, and then proceeded to beat him unmercifully. He was big and strong, and didn't go down easily. The fight lasted many minutes, with all four working on this lone man, at the same time. While this was taking place, a bystander with a video camera, filmed the whole incidence, turning the tape over to the news media. Later when charges were laid, a jury of twelve all white persons, found the policemen, *not guilty,* and set the police free. This of course was unacceptable to the public, and the riots began. We were intrigued by all of this, partly because at this point in our sheltered lives, we had not experienced the high rift between blacks and whites. The other reason was simply that it started near the neighborhood in which Ric lived. The riots began downtown Los Angeles with a break-in of a liquor store. A white trucker was stopped and beaten, then a fire started, and then all was totally out of hand from that point. Of course this was all broadcast minute by minute on colour TV, twenty- four hours a day, and actually went on for weeks on end.

After dark on the first day, hundreds of fires were started, looters became more brazen, and hundreds of stores were broken into with looters carrying off small and large items by the thousands. Police and firefighters from dozens of towns and cities came to help, but still it went on. President Bush called for five thousand military troops to help out, it still continued, with fires, killings, and looting. This didn't stop in Los Angeles alone, it became a racial issue and spread to other large cities, San Francisco, Las Vegas and many other large centers.

Los Angeles looked like a war zone, that couldn't be stopped. All of this because of four policemen getting their jollies, and twelve jurors during the trial that as President George Bush described, "must have been in outer space." Forty-three people lost their lives, over five thousand fires, thousands of people out of work because of the loss of businesses, and damage in excess of five hundred and fifty millions of dollars done, plus millions of dollars in goods stolen. We, of course, had never witnessed anything remotely like this in our little part of the world, but certainly could see how small insignificant things can and do start world wars.

After nearly two weeks of this devastation, it slowed down somewhat, awaiting a new trial, for the black fellow by the name of Rodney King, no relationship to my Connie King, but time for us to travel home. I will say, that in spite of the riots, we did have a wonderful visit with our family.

Home, peaceful home, but was it?

In the early spring, we once again experienced a near drought, and did our usual worrying and extra prayers. Did it work? It sure did, the rains began to come, the crops and gardens rallied, and then shot up beautifully, looking as some of the best ever. Harvest started in the latter part of August and looking good. Then about the 23rd day of August, it turned cold and the snow began to fall, and fall. We had just gone through a week of scorching hot weather. This couldn't last. But the furnace got cranked up, I put on my long sleeve shirt and stared out of the windows. It just kept coming. The full leaf trees began to bend with the weight and then branches began to split and crash to the ground. Our garden flattened, and disappeared from sight under a blanket of heavy wet snow. More trees shattered and broke, it was looking like a different Los Angeles, a grief stricken war zone, only in our once balmy area, no fires, just heavy wet snow covering everything in its wake, and hundreds of trees, gardens and crops smashed beyond description. Thousands of hopes and dreams gone in just hours. Where was God? He was still there, just another big test for this strong and faithful people. As always, we would pick ourselves up and run with it, just as the peoples of Los Angeles must do, just as the peoples of the Philippines, of Iraq and Japan must do.

Three days later we were trimming trees, replacing power lines, hauling piles and piles of branches to a common site to eventually be burned, and farmers trying to salvage what crops they could, or use much of it for cattle feed. During all of this, my father passed away at the age of 86, not a great surprise as his health had been failing and having lots of pain. He put up a great fight and was now blessed to join his *Sweetheart!* We love you Dad!!

Although I have spoken much about my father through the preceding pages, I want to reiterate the fact that he was an exceptional man, challenging many things that he felt were not as they should be. He became involved in provincial politics at quite a young age, which spurred him on to write the paper on banking as he could see it, and as I have mentioned previously, set up the foundation for the now existing Alberta Provincial Treasury Branch, now known as ATB Financial. After acting as an agent for this institution myself for fifteen years, I am sufficiently familiar with the workings, to know that many changes have been made from the original text, many of them *not* good. However, as banks go, it ranks better than most, and certainly is very financially sound. Over the years he held what was called "cottage meetings" to teach others, particularly young persons, about *Monetary Reform,* and did in fact write several books on the subject. He also corresponded with financial people in a variety of countries, including the Secretary Treasurer of the United States. Unfortunately, I was not as sharp of a learner as I should have been, or not as interested as I should have been. The former Provincial Treasurer of Alberta, Ted Hinman, spoke at my dad's funeral, with many glowing remarks and accolades about this man. He achieved much in his lifetime. Our son John also gave a marvellous talk about his grandfather, bringing out some wonderful memories for us to contemplate.

From time to time we lose family and good friends to their eternal progression, and then what is life all about? We know that the reason we come to this sphere of life is to gain a body, have some experiences, some great, while others not so good. Some of us it would seem have to endure this life for a long, long time, while others, just a quick step, but it is difficult for us to understand this when a special loved one leaves us, and we wonder why? Well when we take the time to really look at it, the reasons are all there, we just have to remember and accept, and make it a happy occasion.

The summer that I was called to serve as a Supervisor at the Temple, I felt it would be a wonderful thing for our particular day crew to get together for a special barbeque, thus bringing us closer to one another on a personal basis. All seemed to like the idea, and we planned the first one to be in the backyard of the home of Connie and myself. We made it a potluck with me supplying the steaks. Forty-eight out of the fifty of us attended, having a marvellous time. It went over so well, that we continued this tradition for twelve years at our home, with others later on, sharing in the cost of steaks. Also after the twelve years, we went to the homes of several others for this delightful summer party. After a few years of this, it was decided to add a Christmas get-together for our group as well.

I believe after several years of our crew enjoying these special outings, other Temple groups have also started the tradition, however some of them held in restaurants, not the same intimacy, in my opinion.

I seem to love traditions, and am apt to start something, somewhere with someone. I had purchased a very nice used camper to fit in the box of my truck, and began to think of the best ways to make use of it. Connie was not that keen on camping and so the thing that hit me was to take my grandsons on a camping trip. Wait a minute! That would be quite a crowd, and they were all different ages with a variety of likes and dislikes. I would take them separately, and have a great one on one with each boy, and besides I would get to go more often myself. That is what I planned, and it worked. It did take a few years to get through them all, but they were patient and looked forward to their turn. What a terrific outing with each. Mostly we camped at the same place near a small stream at the Magrath Park. We hiked, we built campfires for wiener roasts, we swam in the stream, and saw lots of deer and other wild animals, birds and fish. It was a beautiful camping spot. I also carved the boy's name on a walking stick for each to use, and keep for a souvenir. With a couple of the boys, we camped at a nice spot near St. Mary's Dam. With Scott, it was the river bottom park near Taber, where we climbed steep hills, and caught frogs, etc. With all, we told stories, chopped wood, and caught minnows. We always had lots to eat, and gained a very special relationship that has lasted all of these many years.

Not to call an end to this close relationship, as the boys got older, in the car, we also did a one on one each year as the boys reached age fourteen. We drove to Wetaskiwin, AB., where we went to a well renowned museum to see antique automobiles, motorcycles, farm machinery and aeroplanes. I took each for a ride in an open cockpit plane. After the museum and trip to a restaurant, we stayed for the night at my sister Cheri and her husband Denis's home for a great visit, barbeque and sightseeing, and then to the famous West Edmonton Mall to swim and go on dangerous rides. Keith, your turn is still yet to come. Some of the boys are now married, but have never forgotten these outings, nor has this Grandpa!!

I have spoken much in the pages of this short account of my life, and given many accolades to my wife with regard to her singing and fine artistry. I have also written a line or two about some of the talents and/or the existence of our older grandchildren. However, I see that I have failed to mention our last and youngest grandson, my namesake, John Keith Hancock Fisher, number six son of John and Kristie. Born in August of 2004, at this point he is ten years of age, has deep brown eyes and dark curly hair; a very handsome and busy young man. He has been in our home lots during his life, mainly because grandma spoils him so much, or at least gives in to his every whim; or perhaps because we live within three blocks of his home and along the route from school to home.

Over these many years grandma has painted an oil portrait on separate canvas of each of our four children and all of our grandchildren with the exception of young Keith, who came along much later than the others. She had decided to give up painting when she felt her eyesight was not as true as it once had been. However, when Keith was about three years of age, he had disappeared silently from view. When I discovered him behind the closed door of the pantry, he had an Oreo cookie in his mouth and both arms loaded with many more of these delicious delicacies. He looked sheepishly at me and stated, "A whole bunch of kukies." I had to smile and take a picture of that sweet moment, with pieces of chocolate cookies smeared all over his impish little face, and small chunks covering his clothing. From that scene, grandma had to paint again.

Home Sweet Home

A FEW YEARS BACK, WE HAD OUR HOME APPRAISED THAT WE MIGHT get a home improvement loan in order to add a bathroom to the second floor, and perhaps a few other improvements. Our home was built in 1925, and although beautiful, well-constructed and for the most part in excellent condition, it did need a little upgrading. The numbers on the appraisal came in high, and upon completion of the appraisal, the appraiser came up with the suggestion that perhaps we should look into having it declared a historic home.

It of course was built for the famed Ray Knight, a multi-millionaire rancher and industrialist. The design of the home was that of the very renowned architect, Frank Lloyd Wright.

These facts of course captured the immediate attention of the Provincial Historic Society, who in turn called me back to arrange for an appointment to view our home. Within a week, I was inundated with several provincial historic personnel, going through every nook and cranny. They were all very impressed, and started the paper work immediately to have it officially declared a Provincial Historic Site. Being somewhat concerned as to what that would mean to me, I was informed that it simply meant that the home could not be torn down (no problem with that), nor could walls be removed. It could be painted, a new roof in the future, windows and doors could be upgraded with their approval. Basically any major change as long as needed and with their authorization, but certainly nothing that would alter the looks or function of the house. Further, that any necessary changes to be made, would be cost shared with me. All pictures and publicity in connection with the new historic declaration would fall under their jurisdiction. It all sounded good to me, and we started immediately by installing thermal pane windows in the basement, and a new hot water boiler in place of the old non-efficient monster that had been a makeover coal burning unit.

Already things were looking up. They also placed a plaque on the front porch, and gave us the name of the "Knight-Hancock Home." In the many succeeding years, a number of pictures of our home have been placed in the museum, and have been written up in magazines and newspapers. We have also had a bus tour of people from Salt Lake City, Utah, Idaho, and other locations, as well, many, many walk- in individuals from a variety of places. We have recently repainted the outside, and replaced the near 90 year old roof with cedar shake shingles. Inside, the dark heavy oak hardwood floors throughout the entire home were refinished to a lighter shade showing the true beauty of the original oak grain. The large living room and den are graced with eleven foot vaulted ceilings, the plaster being embedded with horsehair to prevent any cracking. A first to my knowledge, and it has worked. The living room also features an open-hearth fireplace, as does the master bedroom and basement family room.

Originally, the arched entries into the living room, dining room and den, were enveloped with heavy plush velvet drapes, now fully opened to the foyer with wooden louvered doors entering the den (computer room). The wall sconces and the main chandeliers are of beautiful brass and crystal. Crown mouldings break the walls from the nine foot ceilings in all of the main rooms and halls. The formal dining room served as the eating area for the Knight family, while waited upon by servants.

The home is a six bedroom, three bath, one-and-a-half storey bungalow of approximately six thousand square feet including finished basement and second and main floors. The grounds are immaculate, due to the extent of the forest of trees, shrubs and spacious lawns, planted more than ninety years ago, and subsequently kept up by a lot of hard work and caring by our own busy work, mostly by my hard working wife. It is situated on a one acre lot near the center of town on Park Avenue. The *Carriage House,* as it was originally called, is also one and a half storey matching the house, and was constructed to house two carriages, an ice-house and full food and meat locker, a full compliment of ice, blocked and stored in winter, in the insulated building, and a large office space on the second floor.

In early times, there was a full irrigation system built to adequately care for the entire property. This was done by a series of concrete ditches weaving in and out amongst the lawns and trees. Many of the fruit trees still stand, including apple, and Pottawatomi plum, a pioneer fruit tree, brought into Canada in the early 1900s. Lilac and caragana bushes surround the perimeter of the property.

Our home does not have the luxury of a bath off the master bedroom, but does have a nice four piece across the hall. It has a medium size kitchen, some would like it larger; however, many special people have been entertained with wonderful food from this kitchen. As has been mentioned, the original family of the Ray Knights employed servants to serve them in the spacious dining room, and had no need for a large kitchen.

This truly is a magnificent Historic Home, and as third owners, we are enjoying every square inch of it, and cherish every thought that went into its glorious structure.

Cardston Temple

ONE OF THE MOST INTERESTING AND UNIQUE STRUCTURES TO BE built in Southern Alberta was started in 1914, and completed for use in 1923, was that of the LDS people, The Mormons, known as the Cardston Alberta Temple, constructed of solid granite, and of an Aztec design. The beautiful sparkling whitish grey granite was quarried from a mine near Nelson, British Columbia, and is a spectacle to behold.

I overheard a man one day telling of the location from where the Temple granite was quarried. At this time, I had never given it a thought, but my interest was immediately piqued when he also stated that it still showed plainly and well after these many years. I enquired of him, as to the exact location, he said that he was not sure how to get there, but that it was past Nelson several miles, and on a narrow rarely travelled road. I soon learned that my close friend, Floyd Smith's grandfather, E.J. Wood, had been instrumental with two other men, in locating this fantastic building material for this special building project, a material that would literally stand for a millennium. Floyd said that he and Rula, his wife, would like to travel with my wife and me, to scout out this curious mountain quarry. Before starting this mysterious journey, I did some reading up on the subject, and learned that the mine had been owned by a small group of Serbians. When approached by the Church, they agreed to cut out the size of blocks that was required and have them ready for shipping by barge and rail to the town of Cardston for .55 cents a cubic foot. It was stated that this was a very reasonable rate, and the work began, and took from 1914 to 1918 to complete the job. It took about 350 train cars or approximately three thousand six hundred and ninety tons of granite. The total cost for the granite at that time was $350,000.00, but by today's costs would be in the millions. It was also reported that the Serbian company worked faithfully and hard without any complaining, and therefore the Church sent them a bonus of two thousand dollars, which also would have been a goodly sum at the time.

In our travels to arrive at the quarry, we drove over a beautiful spectacular highway, arriving at a ferry boat to shuttle us across the wide river. On the other side, we did come to a narrow but paved road with steep well treed sides, both above us on the one side, and a long way down on the other, just a bit frightening. When we came to the end of the pavement, seeing nothing that looked like a mine, we drove another five miles, at last seeing a little log cabin a few yards off the main trail. We entered the old log rail gate and encountered an old grizzly looking prospector type of man sitting in a wheelchair. He told us that he had lost both legs in a mining accident many years ago, and that he lived alone, but was still able to chop firewood and otherwise care for himself. We enquired of him, if he knew such a granite mine that we were looking for. He said he knew it well, and that over the years, many people from Salt Lake City and others, had stopped at his cabin to find their way to the mine. We had passed by the entrance about six miles back, just before the pavement ended. I enquired of him, if in fact the narrow highway had once been a rail line, he said that it had been a narrow gage line to the mine, but the tracks had long since been removed and a road built in their place. He also stated that the entrance to the mine was concealed by a lot of brush and trees, but if we watched carefully, we could find it.

Tracing our way back the six miles, we watched carefully, and sure enough, just through some thick bushes, there it stood, magnificently huge. We were all in awe at the size and grandeur of the opening. We had expected to view more of an open pit, rather than this monstrous like cave. It was still adorned with beautiful granite, being able to see where huge blocks had been extracted from the walls and ceiling. It looked large enough to almost sit the Temple back inside the abandoned cave. The only remains were several pieces of large cables and a short strip of narrow gage rail tracks, with a small flatbed rail car resting on them.

We learned that the huge blocks of granite were ultimately shipped to the train station in Cardston, where they were cut to size and shapes as needed, and then loaded on stoneboats to be pulled by large teams of horses up the hill to the building sight. The hill many times was muddy from rain or slippery from winter snows, which made it hard slugging for the horses. The drivers of these teams also had to be very skilled to place these blocks as near as possible for workers to handle.

In small town Alberta, the construction of such an edifice of this magnitude was nothing short of a miracle, while the phenomenal cathedrals throughout Europe and our large cities in North America are completely unbelievable.

The Cardston Alberta Temple built by many unskilled hands, was completed August 26th, 1923 at a final cost of $751,666.53, totally paid before being dedicated and used.

Difficulties and Blessings

PERHAPS THE MOST DAUNTING AND TRAGIC SITUATION TO COME into the lives of our otherwise happy young family was the sudden news of our eldest granddaughter, Shelsi Tenille Hancock, daughter of Ric and Sheri, being afflicted with dreaded cancer. Our former Beauty Queen, then twenty-five years of age and married in the Los Angeles Temple to Eric Stolworthy, being diagnosed with full blown cancer, was almost more than we could handle. Her youngest sister, Kandyse, passed away at three months of age some twenty years previously, and now a second daughter dangerously ill.

Shelsi had a bad cough for some time that couldn't seem to be cured, when after many tests, was found to be lung cancer. A huge growth was found pressing against her heart, making it difficult to remove. A family *Fast* was called for her with many special prayers. The forthcoming Sunday was Stake Conference for their family with Elder Todd Christofferson in attendance, shortly before being called to be an Apostle of the Church; he was approached to give Shelsi a blessing, to which he happily obliged.

In this priesthood blessing, one of the many things that he stated was that her own body would be instrumental in healing itself. We were all grateful for the wonderful blessing that she received, although we didn't know what these particular words meant. She continued on with many, many treatments, and spent several weeks in the Cedar-Sinai

Hospital. She continued on with a positive attitude, even though hurting terribly, she rendered much cheer to others around her, including all of our family members.

One of many persons who stopped in for a visit was the well-known comedian, Brad Garrett, who returned later with a copy of a photo of all of the characters on the show "Everybody Loves Raymond," personally signed by each member of the cast. Shelsi underwent both chemotherapy and radiation, and lost all of her beautiful long blonde hair. Still not to be beat, she participated in a special cancer study program made into a TV documentary for world-wide distribution. She also had a website in which she received more than 50 pages of well-wishers from all over the globe, wishing her well, and offering up their prayers on her behalf. The cancer appeared to be in remission, however, sadly that was not to be.

It was discovered that the cancer had now spread, invading the frontal lobe of the brain, requiring serious surgery. We were all horrified at this news, but Shelsi, being the sweet gentle person that she is, simply said, "This is so annoying."

I sincerely believe that so many prayers had ascended to our Heavenly Father, and so much faith exercised by family, friends and folks in general, that the Lord decided to leave her here. An almost new and somewhat experimental procedure at that time was decided for her. The decision made by her doctors was to extract her own *stem cells*, and use them in the treatment for her cure. The miracle was, the cancer went into remission once again. That has now been nearly eight years ago. When we look back to the wonderful blessing that was given to her by Elder Christofferson, soon after the cancer diagnosis, we now understand what was meant by "your own body will be instrumental in healing itself." That seemed to be the proper answer to her cure. We can never express our gratitude nor tell of our never-ending love.

I believe on the whole, we have experienced more good times than bad, and probably should stick with relating just positive happenings, however, as tragic as it was, Shelsi went through those many months of nerve wracking moments with flying colours.

Summer Fun

THIS LEADS ME TO A VERY FUN FILLED WEEK FOR MANY OF OUR family, camping at Big Bear Lake in the high mountains of California. My sister Dorine and husband Vern had been called to supervise a Church camp for the summer at Big Bear, and had one week in between groups, wherein they could invite their own family to stay for that week. They sent out a call for as many family as could attend. Wow, was that fun! Most of our family were available, and that included our sweet Shelsi and Eric, who were in dire need of that type of relaxation. Along with them, our son Ric attended, as did Jamin his eldest, Andrew and Kira and their two sons, Tony and AJ. Also John J and Kristie and three out of their six sons, Jeff, Jerran and Keith, and of course Connie and myself. This made a total of fifteen from my family, with the entire group totalling more than thirty of us. The camp was set among trees and monstrous boulders. There was a very large hall, bathrooms, kitchen complete with a huge stove, walk-in cooler and sinks, and several cabins also fully equipped for camping. We took family turns at planning and preparing the meals and putting on a program of sorts.

There was never a dull moment for anyone. The kids climbed the huge boulders, the smaller kids scaring us half to death. We also rented a large pontoon boat to roar around the gorgeous crystal blue lake with John Fisher at the helm. The older ones jumped off for a swim under the hot sun and in the warm water. Along the shoreline there were many beautiful homes, many of them in and around the humongous boulders. The total setting was out of a book of dreams. A once in a lifetime vacation, well thought out and well planned.

Another special summer memory came in the form of an honor that I had never thought of or even aspired to consciously. It came out of the blue when proposed that I become the Honorary Parade Marshall for the upcoming Canada Day Parade that is held each First of July in our community. So far it had seemed reserved for some person who had achieved some greatness at a specific calling or was known far and wide for their personal importance, but was formerly from Raymond; or the oldest citizen of the town. I didn't feel I was any of those, however, I knew that I had always worked hard at anything I was asked to do.

It was felt by many that my fighting the government to obtain highway lights and shoulders on our busy highway entering Raymond and serving the town for many years on other matters, that I deserved the honor. I gratefully accepted, and my wife and I were privileged to be escorted on the parade route in a beautiful classic horse-drawn open carriage driven by a renowned driver, Loye Olson, who had driven mayors, the Prime Minister, the Queen, and other noted persons in this same carriage on many occasions. It was quite a thrill for us.

A Blessing and a Miracle

Our beautiful and unique Province of Alberta always keeps us guessing. Even we old timers that have lived here for sixty or eighty years or more don't really know what might come next. We have experienced just about every kind of weather or trauma that could be dished out, from blazing hot sun at over 100 degrees to frigid cold at 50 degrees below zero. Everything from complete drought, tornados and baseball size hail to freezing blizzards and small earthquakes. Our rainstorms can last two to three weeks in one fell swoop, or to gentle life giving moisture. And then there are winds, would you believe some strong enough to completely remove a roof or rip out a ninety year old tree by its well preserved roots. This is *a keep them guessing,* good old beloved Southern Alberta. Now, just where am I going with all of this inside information? Just over one year ago, we experienced the "Flood" of never, ever. The skies of June 19th started clear and sunny, a normal summer day until about six o'clock in the evening, the sky completely blackened, with just a little wind, then picked up quickly with rains coming down in torrents. We had seen this happen many times, however, this didn't want to stop quickly as it had done in most cases. Eighteen to twenty hours later, it was still falling in unprecedented amounts. Two large rivers pass through the city of Calgary, the Bow, and the Elbow, both now beginning to flood their banks. Basements of expensive large homes adjacent to the rivers were taking in water, their yards inundated, the streets and drains could not handle the downpour. Soon other homes and condominiums were flooding, and traffic redirected. Downtown Calgary was soon a nightmare. The world famous Stampede Grounds, tracks, barns, and grandstands were beginning to fill up rapidly. What could be done with the *Greatest Outdoor Show on Earth,* less than a month away? Millions of tourists from all parts of the world plan, some for years ahead, to attend this magnificent event. The water was now up to the fourteenth row of seats, and of course all of the arenas, chutes and tracks were under water. The city was looking at millions of dollars in losses if the show didn't go on, as well as the merchants in town. To say nothing of the thousands of homes damaged or destroyed. The peoples of Calgary are resilient and resourceful and thousands of volunteers went to work draining, sandbagging, and hauling in thousands of tons of sand and gravel, to make amends, and the *Show did go on!*

Worse hit than the city of Calgary, only on a smaller scale, because of the size, was the town of High River some thirty miles south of Calgary. It was nearly totally inundated, private homes and businesses. Many newer homes recently constructed, hotels, stores and the like. The town had taken a huge growth in recent years and was essentially a *New Town.* The area had to be evacuated completely, with the residents moving in with family and friends for weeks at a time. The water was so deep and came so suddenly that families were not prepared, and many had to be rescued in the back of huge dump trucks, fire engines and boats. Unfortunately about five people lost their lives in the skirmish. The Provincial Government finally brought in many hundreds of mobile home units to house people. When driving past High River on the double lane highway, looking over to the town weeks later, basically you could see only roofs of buildings rising above the sea of water. Many volunteers from nearly every town or city in the province attended the town to help slog out basements, stores and streets. Other communities such as Bowness, Siksika Nations, Bragg Creek and Canmore were also struck hard by the flooding. Countless millions of dollars in damage hit these communities. Any place that had a river running through or nearby were hit hard with rivers and streams rising quickly and overflowing their banks.

This has been a year of disasters the likes of which we have never seen in past decades. These disasters appear to be taking place throughout all parts of the world. Many earthquakes, tornados, hurricanes, fires, floods and tsunamis are striking without mercy. Sadly enough a major share of the Middle East countries are at war. Russia is trying very hard to take over the Ukraine, if they do succeed, they will soon follow suit with other small countries. The West is trying hard to stop this. Will they succeed ????

A Very Special Fiftieth Wedding Anniversary -Our Anniversary Trip 50 Years of Excitement and Trials September 29, 1956 - 2006

"**September 8, 2006:** A beautiful and sunny fall day to start a trip of a lifetime. Many of our closest and dearest friends celebrated their Golden Wedding Anniversaries with a huge get together party of family and friends, however my dear companion preferred a trip of some sort rather than stand in the traditional lineup eating Jello salad and ham buns, washed down with red punch and a brownie.

Now to the fun and awesome thirty day trek. Our son-in-law, John Fisher, drove us to Shelby, Montana, where we met the Amtrack train, a first for both of us. I have travelled much by train throughout the years of my mission, however Connie had never been on one, so it was exciting for both of us. The Amtrack is comfortable and fast, equipped with observation car, a dining car, and plush seats. Most stops were but a few minutes to allow for boarding and disembarking of passengers.

The scenery was remarkable and in particular around the Great Lakes. After a half comfortable sleep, our first lengthy stop was twenty-seven hours later at the famous Union Station in Chicago.

Here we changed trains after a three-hour layover, and soon another night of sleep in our seats. This time I slept a little better, and full of anxious anticipation to begin our real vacation trip. This was a Sunday morning at about 10:00 A.M. We took a taxi from the train station at Rochester, N.Y., to the airport where we had a rental car waiting for us. No hassle at all. It was a nice silver Chev Impala, very comfortable, zippy, and fairly easy on gas.

The town of Palmyra was only about 16 miles from Rochester and easy to locate on the map. Our first stop was at the Church Visitor Center located on the Joseph Smith farm approximately six miles out of Palmyra. Our visit there was quite short, as we needed to find a motel or some sort of lodging for the night. We were informed that there was a Sister Baldorf just on the other edge of Palmyra who rented rooms to LDS people. We drove on out and got settled in to a basement room. It wasn't particularly nice, but we felt that it would work for us as there didn't seem to be a motel close around with exception of the Palmyra Inn which was over $100 per night, well over our budget.

After settling in, we drove around the town, finding something to eat and taking in a few sights. Located on each of four corners of an intersection there were huge very old churches, founded in the early 1800s. They call it the corner of the four churches, each church being massive. We found Palmyra to be quite a large community, unlike what I had always understood.

By this time it was getting early evening with a beautiful sunset. In my hurry to take a picture of the church steeples looming up into the sun's rays, I tripped on a sidewalk curb and badly injured an elbow, hip and hand. The bone in my elbow was visible with lots of bleeding; my hip turned all the colors of the rainbow. As this was our first day, we thought our trip to be ruined for sure. However after some Polysporin and bandaging we were back in business. It was uncomfortable for about ten days, but did not slow us down from our touring and fun. When we awakened the first morning, we were delighted to view the well-known Erie Canal running adjacent to the back yard of where we were staying, it was quite a magnificent sight. The sightseeing had begun.

We grabbed a quick bite to eat and then drove to the Martin Harris farm. It was not opened to the public, but was a beautiful home built of lake stones held together with a cement type of mortar. The landscaping in the area was beautiful with acres of cornfields, and thousands upon thousands of lush green fields, shrubs and trees. For us old prairie dogs, it was a sight to behold. We then drove downtown Palmyra to the Grandin building where the Book of Mormon was first printed.

The Church had missionaries stationed there to take you on a tour. I felt myself reverting back more than 175 years ago to the first printing, while walking on the original flooring of the print shop, where Joseph had actually walked. The tour was informative and great, learning of the old methods used in type setting and printing. Five thousand copies were first printed here and bound in pigskin leather. In my estimation, "What a feat!" Our next stop of course was to the Joseph Smith Farm Visitor Centre where we met with some wonderful missionaries who took us on a tour and explanation of the Smith cottages.

I took many pictures as we looked in awe. Much of the first cottage and furnishings were replica, but there were some pieces and boards from the original. A wonderful and spiritual feeling was present and a definite strengthening of testimony as we walked and talked.

The second home, called the frame home, built by Alvin, Joseph's older brother for the parents, was mostly original and restored. Speaking of Alvin, we viewed his gravesite and tombstone located in Palmyra. He died at a young age, but was very important and prevalent in the life of Joseph and the Smith family.

We then walked through the awesome Sacred Grove where Joseph knelt and prayed as a young boy of 14 years and received a visitation of the Father and the Son. What an indescribable feeling this was; what a strengthening of our personal testimonies to reflect on this true and sacred happening, and in knowing that we are heirs to this great and wonderful restored Gospel. Our second day was complete, and all we could contain and fathom for one day. A little more driving around the area and supper at a Greek Restaurant, very good food and the price was right.

The following day started out a bit cloudy, but soon turned into another lovely day for sightseeing and touring these awesome historic Church sites. Our first stop today was just another few miles from the Smith farm, the Hill Cumorah, a quick pause at the Visitor Centre and then a drive to the top of the Hill where we parked and then walked on over to the monument of the Angel Moroni with plaques of the three and the eight witnesses to the Book of Mormon. The hill is adorned with beautiful small and large trees thickly filled in with pretty shrubbery. One side of the hill overlooks acres of lush green lawns where the annual Pageant takes place with seating for thousands, a phenomenal undertaking every July. One day we also would like to see this wonderful portrayal of Joseph's vision of our Savior. After basking in the thrill of this site, we returned to the Visitor's Center and once again viewed the wonderful film of "Joseph Smith, the Prophet" which now had a much keener meaning to us.

Still early in the day, we then drove to Fayette Township to the farm of Peter Whitmer, another beautiful area, where the Church was organized on April 6, 1830. A large Church Visitor Center has been constructed on this site where very knowledgeable missionaries are posted. We toured the site and walked through the restored but original cottage of 1830. Viewing all of these fascinating sites and traversing the same floors and paths that our beloved prophet and our pioneer forefathers traversed is so very awe-inspiring that words cannot describe nor tongue tell of the keenness of testimony that grows within your mind and spirit.

We completed our day full of awesome wonder and ready for a little life giving sustenance, rest and relaxation preparing for another busy day.

Wednesday September 13th having no special plans, we drove to an area a little further down the road to find a huge store called Wegmans, part of a grocery store chain. We had never experienced a store like this one, all items in the store were placed immaculately on the shelves. All labels were facing the same direction and placed in proper order of the product. I have never encountered such a variety of products, nor so many of each. It truly was the largest grocery store that I have ever seen, and certainly the cleanest and most orderly. It seems to be well known in the East and very popular.

We were told somewhere in our travels about a store located at Naples N.Y. where Grape Pies were made, and that there was nothing quite like them for taste. Out of curiosity and a yearning for something special, we followed our maps once again to find this place which is located at the southern tip of Lake Canadaigua, one of the five Finger Lakes which are south of the Great Lakes. It was in a beautiful wooded area right close to the highway. Not a large bakery, but over the years has become quite famous for pie making and shipping to many places in the east, but their specialty was pie made with Concord grapes, grown in the area. "Monica's Pies" has been written up in several magazines of distinction. We bought a whole pie to take back to the motel with us, and was it ever delicious.

The following day was a bit dreary as it rained all day. We spent this day driving in the area and stopping at the Visitor Center for a while, wrote some more post cards and a couple of birthday cards, and in general just relaxed.

Friday started out somewhat overcast, but did get sunnier as the day wore on. This day we decided to drive to Niagara Falls to see this world famous site. It was less than a two hour drive with more beautiful scenery as we drove. What a magnificent sight. We parked our car and walked a trail to the falls where we took lots of pictures. We then purchased tickets for a trip on the Maid of the Mist to go just below the falls. That was a thrill of a lifetime, getting soaked with the spray and sailing just below and immediately in front of this wonder of wonders. The thunderous roar and massiveness of the falls above was almost unfathomable. It certainly was one of the highlights of our trip. By the time we returned to our room in Palmyra, it was dark and pouring rain, and to complicate things more, we found that two more couples had moved into small rooms next to ours, and would share the one small bathroom, the little kitchenette, and T.V. They seemed to be nice folks, but it was just too much for us. We never were that excited over the accommodations at best and this certainly did not improve things. It was ten o'clock at night and raining hard, but we packed up and went looking for a motel elsewhere. We located one about 15 miles out of Palmyra at a town called Farmington. The price was somewhat higher, but private and much more suitable to our needs. We stayed here four nights before moving on.

The Sunday 17th we attended all of our Church services at the Palmyra Stake Center and later drove around to several other important Church sites in the area. We even found a small city called Fisher, and were quite impressed with beauty of the area and the big homes there as well as the older long before established places. We also took the time to see the "Joseph Smith" film one more time at the Cumorah Visitor Center.

The next day of course was Monday and normally the Temple would be closed; however, it had been closed for two weeks for cleaning, and was opened on the Monday for sessions. The Palmyra Temple is small but as all Temples, is very beautiful set in a grove of trees overlooking the Smith farm and the Sacred Grove, another site almost too sacred to tell about. The officiators were so very nice and accommodating to us. We loved the experience.

Tuesday morning we checked out and left early to travel to Kirtland, Ohio, about a four-and-a-half hour drive. Another awesome drive through unbelievable scenery. In Pennsylvania there were miles of grape vineyards as well as trees. We found ourselves driving very close to Lake Erie, and left the highway to explore a small country road leading to the shores of this grand lake. It was almost like seeing the ocean, it was so huge. Grape vineyards grew right down to the edge of the foaming shores. When standing out of the car, the fragrance of the grapes was overwhelming and large clusters of grapes dripped down from the vines. We couldn't help but taste a few of them. Pennsylvania truly was our favorite state for its magnificent beauty.

Once again, our first stop when arriving at the city of Kirtland was at the Church Visitor Center. They directed us to the Red Roof Inn where we discovered that they gave a good discount to Church members. It was new and exceptionally clean and quite close to the church sites. We checked in and then found a Wendy's restaurant close by for a good meal. We found that a Wendy's or MacDonald's had the best meals for the price, and thus ate at a lot of them on our trip.

We had an interesting experience the following day as we shopped for groceries in quite a large grocery store. We put on a change of clothes and didn't look quite so grubby as while travelling, when a lady customer said, "Oh you look so nice, I should dress up a little better when I come shopping."

It was such a nice compliment that Connie struck up a conversation with her. She was very receptive to the conversation and did listen intently as Connie told her somewhat of our trip and how the Church entered in to our tour.

Connie gave her some "pass along cards" and told her a bit about our church. She said that years ago some missionaries had given her a Book of Mormon, but she had not read it. Her name was Jean Davis, and Connie almost felt that she was a long lost sister. They said goodbye and waved at each other as we left our respective checkout counters. We both feel that she will in-fact contact the Church sometime in the near future.

I am pleased to say that on this vacation trip, Connie had passed along a couple dozen of these cards.

We returned to the Visitor Centre and did a tour of the immediate area, including the old Saw Mill, the Ashery and the Chagrin River where many baptisms took place including that of my great-grandfather, Solomon Hancock. We then drove to the Stone Quarry where the sandstone was obtained to build the Kirtland Temple.

The next day was bright and sunny, and our first visit for the day was a short jaunt to the Isaac Morley farm. I hadn't realized how very significant this place was. There had been an old schoolhouse up a wooded trail from the house where a meeting was held by the Prophet Joseph with several men in attendance to receive the Melchizedek Priesthood. They were attacked by powers of Satan, and wrestled with the blackness most of the night. In early morning Heavenly Father and Jesus Christ appeared to eradicate this power and set things straight.

This incident is all documented, and one of the important things to me was the fact that my great-grandfather, Solomon, and his brother Levi Hancock, were in attendance when this took place. When our guide told us of this, I was quite shaken and in awe. We went from this place to visit the Kirtland Temple, which is now owned by the Community of Christ church and used as a tourist site. We of course were impressed by the Temple, but not particularly by the tour guide. It just didn't quite fit. I believe the time is not too far away when it will be back into the hands of our Church for restoration and use as a working Temple.

It was still early in the day, so we decided to drive to the John Johnson Farm, yet another important Church history site. This was in the area referred to as Hiram where many of the revelations that are recorded in the Doctrine and Covenants took place; it is also the home that Joseph and Emma were living in when the Prophet was dragged out of bed by assailants and was tarred and feathered by the mob and where one of the babies died of exposure because of this cruel act.

Most of this home and contents are original. Our missionary guide did a tremendous job of telling of the many things that took place here. My great grandfather Solomon also spent time at this place being schooled by the Prophet in things pertaining to the Gospel.

It was awesome to walk on the same floors and in the same rooms where these things took place nearly 200 years ago.

On our way back to Kirtland, we stopped to eat at an Amish restaurant, Mary Yoder's, great food and very interesting. We saw quite a few Amish buggies, with their beautiful high stepping horses, along the highway and on the streets of the communities.

Friday September 22nd, we visited again with Elder and Sister James at the Centre, a couple that we enjoyed visiting with, and then drove to Fairport Harbor, a place where many Saints landed, travelling from Palmyra on the Erie Canal to Lake Erie and to this harbor near Kirtland, Ohio.

Saturday was a day of travelling, once again through picture perfect countryside with lots of Amish folks in the area. There were nice farms and houses, beautiful groves of trees starting to change to fall colors. Leaving the main highway, we found a picturesque covered bridge leading to an area of restored and original old buildings, sort of a museum place or old fort. We took quite a few pictures there before continuing on our way. The place was called Bedford, Pennsylvania. We somehow missed a turn going through a town, but came to a little ice cream store where they had homemade ice cream. We bought huge cones that were the smoothest and best ice cream we had ever eaten. That night we stopped at Somerset, Pennsylvania. I was too tired to drive further.

We stayed at a nice motel that included breakfast the next morning. Later in the morning we came to a small city in Maryland, called Hancock, a must for us to stop. We drove up and down Main Street seeing "Welcome to Hancock" signs. We stopped at a park by a Historic Large old Canal, bought gas and groceries, and moved on.

We arrived in Washington, DC at about four in the afternoon and hit lots of traffic. Being a Sunday we could imagine just what the traffic would be like on a working day.

With maps, Connie soon got us to the Temple site. Wow what a sight that was! We did see it about twenty- eight years previous when we picked up Ric from his New York mission, but with the six magnificent towers looming out of the trees, it had the same impact on us as before. It truly appeared to be something out of this world.

The location is on the edge of the city in a community called Kensington, Maryland.

We drove to the Visitor Centre on the Temple grounds wondering if there would be anyone around on a Sunday, but found that to be one of their busiest days. We were welcomed most graciously by several Sister missionaries, and wasn't long until we were seated watching the "Joseph Smith the Prophet" film, once again. The theatre there is as large as the Legacy theatre in Salt Lake.

We then asked if they knew of a place to stay that would be reasonable, the hotels/motels were all near or over the $100.00 range, however, there was a Brother and Sister Hanson about a block away that sometimes rented out a room in their grand old home.

A phone call later, we were at their door, a beautiful older home with a room and a bath on the second floor for only $35.00 per night. We were in awe, and found them to be former Temple workers, and he being a Sealer in the Washington Temple. Brother Walter Hanson was 93 and Sister Helen Hanson 87 years of age, and wonderful people. We stayed with them for three nights, visited with them in depth and became quite close friends before our stay was over.

Monday morning we parked our car at the Metro Station and went into the city for a tour of the sites on a tour bus. The bus stopped at many historic locations or slowly passed them, with a running report as to what they were. We could have gotten off at a number of places and then wait for another bus, but would not have gotten all the way through the tour. We did get off at the Lincoln Memorial for a more in-depth look and found that to be quite a thrill.

On the tour the narrator did talk about John Hancock the signer in very lengthy and glowing terms, an exciting thing for me. The name of "Hancock" is so very well known in the East, and is as famous and well respected as is Abraham Lincoln. All over the city, the name of Hancock was on a street, a building or a plaque. I am proud to carry that name, and hope that I will always uphold it and do it honor.

The days had beautiful warmth and sunshine, we took many pictures and attended two sessions at the Temple. We also had a great visit with the Hansons, getting to know them even better.

Brother Hanson was set apart several years ago as a Sealer in the Washington Temple by President Hinckley. As the two of them conversed, President Hinckley said to him, "Brother Hanson, you were in the Forestry Service for many years. Tell me, is there anything that can be done to save my black walnut trees that are dying?"

Brother Hanson said, "No I am afraid not. When they start to die, they cannot be brought back, but may I suggest that since these have such beautiful wood that you call a wood working expert and have them cut and treated to save the wood, and then have something special made from them." Well as we know, that is exactly what the President did, and consequently the beautiful pulpit that stands in the new Conference Center is constructed of the gorgeous wood from those black walnut trees out of the back yard of President Hinckley's home. I remember at the dedication of this center when President Hinckley said, "I am standing by my tree in this beautiful new building."

We returned to the Visitor Centre for more touring, ate a meal at the Temple and another at Wendy's and then sat down with maps to plan our next travels on the morrow. What a fun and glorious trip this was for us, and so relaxing without the cares at home, nor even knowing what is going on back there for that matter. We just hoped and prayed that all was well.

September 27 we again took leave for more interesting travels. It had not been our intention to stop at Gettysburg in Pennsylvania, however we found ourselves within thirty miles of this historic place and felt that we should drive over to see what it was all about.

Last year we saw the movie "Gettysburg" and were very impressed with it. Well, what a stop that was; one of the highlights of our travels. It has become a real tourist town, teeming with visitors, curio shops and all that goes with it. We were able to do our own tour, taking pictures of 200 year old buildings and landmarks. After an hour or so in the town itself we drove out to the area of the battlefield, stopping first at a museum, cemetery and huge monuments in a park, erected by each state in the Union in memory of their fallen soldiers in that horrific battle. It was extremely interesting to us, however the big amazing story for us was when we drove on out to the actual battlefield.

The main thoroughfare through this site was called Hancock Avenue named for Major General Winnfield Scott Hancock, one of the more prominent Generals in the war. We also beheld a huge monument to the battle (double the size of most homes) adorned with a large statue on each corner, one of which was Abraham Lincoln, another was that of Major General Winnfield Scott Hancock. We were almost speechless to see this as he is one of our ancestors.

There were many other names of soldiers on the various plaques, a number of Hancocks that fought and died in this great battle. Interestingly while I viewed the monument from ground level, a couple who were also touring said that they came out there several times a year, had seen the movie "Gettysburg" a number of times and had read books and articles by the dozen with regard to this battle. They indicated to me that General Hancock was their greatest hero, and when I said to them that I was a Hancock and that he was an ancestor they both shook my hand vigorously, called me sir, and asked if he could take a picture of me standing by his wife and told me that it was such an honor to meet me.

I was more than a little amazed and flattered by all of the attention I was receiving. They proceeded to tell Connie and me stories of General

Hancock and requested our address. As I mentioned earlier in this writing, the name of "Hancock" is so very well-known and revered in the Eastern part of the States.

The overview of the battlefield with all of its rock walls; bunkers, fences, statues and plaques was humbling and left us in awe knowing that Joseph Smith had predicted this very war several years before it took place. We spent several hours there and felt that it was one of the more interesting and spiritual stops that we had made. We travelled on marveling at the beauty of the countryside, the old barns, the trees, acres and acres of cornfields and pumpkins and more Amish settlements.

So very picturesque is the State of Pennsylvania that one must actually see it to take it all in. Every corner, every valley, every farm is a picture by itself. Drawing dusk, we looked for a motel and a place to eat. We stopped at a place called Lebanon Valley at a Best Western, with a Wendy's across the street, our nicest hotel yet. It also included a very nice breakfast. Still in the State of Pennsylvania on the following day, we came to a very nice rest stop. While there I picked up a brochure whilst Connie was busy getting acquainted with a lady and giving her a "pass along" card as she had done so much of (she is a regular missionary). After driving down the highway several miles, I handed her the brochure and said, "See if there is anything of interest in there."

When she opened it up, the first thing to pop out at her was a note about a Mormon statue in the area. She said to turn off at exit 171. We both looked up and saw that it was almost on us. I quickly signaled to get off and to our amazement it was just ten miles down the road to a place called Susquehanna and adjacent to that river.

As it turned out, it was the Church marker of the restoration of the Aaronic Priesthood, a beautiful bronze statue of Joseph and Oliver receiving the priesthood by John the Baptist. The grounds were very well maintained with lawns and flowers and a cemetery next to it containing the graves of Emma's parents, Isaac and Elizabeth Hale, and that of the first born son of Joseph and Emma. We had always believed this place to be called Harmony, (now called Oakland) but that in fact was the name of the county and the place where the Prophet Joseph first began the translating of the Book of Mormon from the Sacred Plates, and Emma received the mandate to be the scribe for her husband in the translation. There had been a small cabin near here where they lived, but no longer a sign of it. We continued on our way feeling excited that we found this important site.

We also passed Bainbridge, where Joseph worked for Isaac Stohl. That evening after a long drive we arrived at a place called Cobleskill, a very small town in New York near the State of Vermont. We noticed that the trees were beginning to change to their fall colors and this made for a beautiful drive, only that by this time of day, it was beginning to rain fairly hard.

Not wishing to push ourselves any later in the day with the rain, we called it a day for our driving. We stayed at a Super 8 motel and ate at a nearby MacDonald's.

September 29th, the day of our 50th Anniversary; this was the day that this trip was all about, so it should be the best day of our travels. Well we did have some special experiences and I hope that I can tell them accurately and able to remember the feelings and things that took place on this our special day.

The day started out rainy and cool unlike our wedding day which was a marvelous bright and sunny fall day fifty years ago. Somehow this weather didn't detract from the uncanny scenery of beautiful Vermont. In this area it was mountainous and extremely forested; the highway was in perfect condition and rose above most of the communities and open tracts of land, revealing the magnificent beauties of nature with a little help from mankind to take us through the center of all of this unspoiled terrain.

Throughout our entire trip in each of the States in the east, we noticed how the thousands of acres of grass and hay were mowed to perfection whether it be on farms or along the highways or at private homes. I am sure I have never witnessed such greenery. Our Heavenly Father certainly did produce a gorgeous world for us to reside on, if we would just take the responsibility to care for it. To take us further into this special day, we arrived at Sharon, Vermont, a small community but clean and neat. We found that the birthplace of the prophet was about 10 or 12 miles out of town on a farm. The road was paved and not difficult to find. We arrived about 5:30 in the afternoon to the Church Visitor Center. It was getting dusk and a light cool rain falling. We asked a gentleman if there was an Elder Williams there. He said that he was the man and in charge of the Center. We explained that we had met Ron Adamson at Albany, in New York, and that he had told us to look for Elder Williams and that he would look after us.

Well he was not the friendliest missionary that we had ever met, but invited us into the large home that was provided for the missionaries. We further stated that we did not have a motel booked and could he help us out. He said that because of this time of year there were thousands of tourists in the area (leaf huggers) people who come for the changing of the fall leaves to their beautiful brilliance of reds, oranges and yellows, etc. This was somewhat of a novelty to us. We had heard that many people came for this season, but didn't realize that it was in the thousands. The motels were booked solid except for two, which the cost per night was toward $179.00. Our budget didn't allow for this kind of money, and we said that we would probably have to sleep in the car. He still didn't offer us shelter when Connie bravely said, "If it were me, I would say come sleep on the floor." No response. Finally he said maybe there is one other choice. He made a phone call and then explained to us that there was in-fact a girls' summer camp down the road two miles which was owned by the Church and was called Camp Joseph. We could sleep in a cabin there.

He loaned us two light summer type sleeping bags and two pillows. There was no heat nor lights in the cabin. I had a flashlight in the car, and we found the place with tiny log cabins, concrete floor, a small window on one end and two sets of narrow bunk beds with a mattress. By this time it was completely dark, very cold and rainy. It wasn't the most welcome sight that I had ever encountered, but would keep us dry from the rain and/or snow if it came.

Of course we were in the mountains as beautiful as they were. We crawled into the sleeping bags with our clothes and jackets, only removing our shoes. Wow, was it cold! I could tell that Connie could not make it through the night, and remembered that we had two small blankets in the car that we carried with us on the train. I put shoes back on and brought them back for Connie to tuck inside her sleeping bag. She began to insist that 1 take one of them. Of course I stated that I would be okay and for her to use them both. She knew that I would not give in, and snuggled into them for a fairly warm night. Well I have never been that cold in all of my life for so many hours. It was only about seven at night with about twelve hours ahead of us.

Where the eaves joined the side walls, there a six inch space for the wind to blow cold air in on me. My feet were like two blocks of ice and my nose an icicle. I turned from side to back all night long and seemed to look at my watch every twenty minutes to half hour. About five o'clock I thought I should go sit in the car and warm up, and then I would remember our pioneers went through so much worse than that, that I surely could survive one night in the cold.

Connie said she kept thinking "No room in the Inn" and contented herself with that thought. About seven in the morning, I said this is enough. I got up and opened the door with a view of more than an inch of frost on everything. It had gotten below freezing. However, my woes soon turned to overwhelming joy and gratitude when I beheld the most beautiful sight that I had ever seen. The sun was coming up over the mountains and shining through the trees and a heavy mist. I never had seen the likes of it. Connie and I both shouted for joy and felt that was probably one of the greatest experiences of our lives.

Our car was parked in front of a large apple tree and orchard that was loaded with huge juicy red apples ready for the picking. We did pick a few for breakfast and a few more to take with us. After the car heater warmed us up and melted the icy windows, we drove back to the Visitor Center. There was a drive of several hundred yards up a lane to get there. On either side of the lane were very large sugar maple trees that had been planted more than 100 years previous. The sun was also shining through a heavy mist and through the trees as we ventured on. An absolute heavenly sight. We almost expected the Savior to appear. It was that ethereal and awe inspiring. To me it was indeed a second Sacred Grove. What an adventure for the night of our Fiftieth Wedding Anniversary.

We also very much enjoyed the Visitor Centre and the monument to Joseph Smith. The obelisk is 38.6 feet tall signifying one foot for each year of his young life. It consists of one piece of solid granite set on two large bases. There is a great story connected with getting it there which I won't go into at this time. We also saw in the heavy wooded area, a stone bridge covered with moss with a pretty little creek running under it. It was fascinating to us knowing that our prophet had stood on and crossed it many times.

It was a beautiful sunny morning a Saturday, with General Conference being broadcast a little later. We made a decision to drive back to Palmyra in order for us to take in the two Sunday sessions the following day. We couldn't attend all four so this was for the best.

Once again a wonderful drive back, stopping to see a covered bridge and take a few pictures along the way. It was a very long drive back to Palmyra, and before we got back, we hit the heaviest rain of our trip, almost to the point of no visibility. We arrived at Farmington where we had stayed for four nights but found the motel to have no vacancy.

Closer to Palmyra was the Palmyra Inn with one vacancy but was very expensive for us, $101.00. After the night before in the cabin, we felt we needed an extra nice place to get cleaned up for Sunday General

Conference. It also included a super nice breakfast and was located just around the comer from the Stake Centre where conference was to be broadcast.

October 1st, the birth date of a precious granddaughter who passed from this life at the age of three months, pure and undefiled by this precarious life. She would have been 19 years of age this year.

We will be with you before too much longer, my dear little Kandyse, and will rejoice with you through the Eternities.

Well as always we enjoyed the counsel of the Brethren and as always, we particularly enjoyed the words of wisdom from our beloved Prophet, President Hinckley. At the age of 97 he was still stalwart and strong with a tremendous sense of humor. Our faith and prayers were continually with you, dear Prophet. We moved back to our little motel in Farmington, about 15 miles out of Palmyra, where we stayed five more nights, the remainder of our stay in the East.

Monday was a beautiful fall day after all of the refreshing rain that we had experienced, and we felt that we should spend some more time in the Sacred Grove while we were nearby. This time for some reason, it felt more like we hoped it would be the first time through. We entered from the opposite end of the Grove and walked different paths, and this time we took a lot of time pondering the event of the young boy Joseph. We sat on several of the benches and fallen trees as we strolled through the serene and beautiful woods taking in the quietude that we beheld.

It was a fresh morning, and the birds were literally singing as the song tells. Our thoughts and feelings were magnified and once again our testimonies strengthened as to the truthfulness of the Gospel. We were so happy to have had this second opportunity to submerge ourselves into this awe inspiring place in history. It now means so very much more to me; another marvelous experience.

Speaking of experiences, an interesting thing happened to us later in this day as we were shopping for some groceries in a store. I walked down an aisle and almost jumped out of my skin. I found Connie and said, "I just saw your dad!" We went back to that same aisle and then she was just about bowled over. The man we saw was the spitting image of Harold King. He had the same indented nose, same forehead and bald head, same type of clothes Dad King wore. Even walked the same. We had a hard time not just staring or going up to talk with him. If everyone has a double, that man was his.

We relaxed in our motel that evening and planned our next few days. Tuesday morning we attended the Palmyra Temple, going through a session, and were called to be the witnesses for the session. We also met once again, Sister Marsha Calder, who is counselor to the Matron. We became very good friends with her and her husband Doug. Connie gave her a copy of the painting of President Hinckley that Connie had done, also a copy of a CD that Connie had made. She gave us a copy of a CD that her husband had made. We exchanged addresses. They live in Salt Lake and would be released November 1st. Marsha was very beautiful and looked a lot like Connie in many ways. They invited us to come stay with them when we are in Salt Lake next.

Once again we drove to the Hill Cumorah where we saw the Joseph Smith film for the fourth time. It got better each time we saw it. Perhaps because we had visited so many sacred places where the Prophet dwelt. Wednesday we went through one more Temple session, our fifth one on this vacation trip, two in DC and three at the Palmyra Temple. Thursday morning we cleaned the car inside and out in readiness to return it the next day. We then decided to drive around the area one more time, driving to the cities of Fisher and Meriden. We came upon another community called Pittsford; we loved this city, pretty good size and just beautiful. The Erie Canal runs through the middle of it, and a large area downtown is a real tourist haven. Apparently it was an important port for the canal. Very picturesque wherever you look, and beautiful old homes. We spent several hours in this place.

All in all, for our last day, it made for a wonderful drive, including taking pictures of some trees that had changed colors. We took our time driving through the countryside, including some farming areas before returning to our motel for one more night's sleep.

Friday morning, October 6th, was our day to return the rented car to Rochester Airport and we felt a little saddened to be coming to the end of a perfect vacation, but then we were getting a little homesick to see our kids and we especially missed our little Keifer (Keith). We had become so attached to this little fellow that we talked about him constantly on our trip. Yes, we did miss all of our grand kids, but they were getting grown up and seemed to be looking after themselves pretty well, while Keith changed every day and learned more every time we didn't see him for a couple of days. To be away for a month, we know there would be a big change.

We returned the car just before noon and then went for something to eat in the airport when I said, "Where is my camera? Still in the car!"

We rushed back to the rental place where they phoned the drop off spot, where it was reported that it was in-fact in the car. What a relief that was, as we had taken more than six hundred pictures. We wasted no time in retrieving it with a great huge sigh of gratitude.

We then had a ten-hour wait before our train was to arrive. We took a taxi back into the city, going directly to the Eastman Kodak Museum where we spent four-and-a-half hours. It was a seventy-five room mansion where George Eastman lived as a bachelor with his mother who had her own suite upstairs. We went on a tour and learned many interesting things. George Eastman was the inventor of the famous Brownie camera that he wanted to sell cheaply enough that every kid could own one. We learned that this famous man committed suicide at age 76, stating that "My work is finished, why wait?"

Speaking of waiting, after returning to the train station where we had left our luggage before returning the car, we had nothing to do but wait for another five hours. We were excited to have the train arrive. It was almost sleep time and that is pretty well what we did until we arrived in Chicago.

A layover for several hours in that huge city gave us time to eat dinner and explore the city a bit. I went out to the streets where I took quite a number of pictures of the magnificent tall buildings, the canal and boats, and people on the streets.

Our train from Chicago to Shelby was a fairly new coach and was real luxury by comparison to the others we had been on. We loved sightseeing as we went along, and thoroughly enjoyed each other's companionship. It was fun eating a good meal in the dining car, sitting in the observation car and looking at some well-known cities as we travelled on. Gary, Indiana, was quite a surprise to us to see what a huge industrial area it was, miles and miles and miles of factories mostly old and pollutant but still in service. I can hardly imagine so much steel and brick. I don't know what they manufacture but it looks like half the stuff in North America must be built there.

After many hours of watching out of the windows, reading, etc., darkness finally prevailed. I should mention that once again Connie did her missionary work. She talked to a lot of people about the Church and gave them information cards, etc. She is a real little trooper and would serve a great mission if she were called to do so. I in turn am quite a dud in this area.

We went to sleep watching beautiful treed scenery with lakes and rivers and greenery everywhere, and woke up in North Dakota.

Wow what a change. Knowing that this is a lot like the area that we reside in made us scratch our heads and ask WHY!!!!! It was flat, dry, and wind-blown, with nothing wonderful to look at for hundreds of miles. The farm buildings and little towns that we passed by were shabby and very unkempt. Well Alberta certainly wasn't that bad, and we do have some nice areas, but it sure wasn't like the East coast. But I don't think that most of us would trade those folks for anything. We sure are a bunch of Prairie Dogs.

We arrived in Shelby, Montana, about 4:30 in the afternoon and were excited to greet our son-in-law, John Fisher. He is a good and kind man, and we love him dearly.

The short trip home from there was informative but uneventful, and when we did arrive our sweet Kristie Lee with some help from her boys, and sister Lisa Jill, had a beautiful Thanksgiving Dinner awaiting us, turkey and all of the trimmings, and a whole lot of love ...

I could almost have typed this account up with one less sheet of paper, but before I sign off, I want to say how very much I enjoyed this wonderful, wonderful time with the love of my life, my darling eternal wife and phenomenal companion. What an absolute joy it is to be with her, to share thirty days of sheer wonderment and friendship. That is to say nothing compared to our fifty years of trials and tribulations, but over and above that, which we don't need to dwell on, is the fifty years of *excitement and ecstasy.* I love you so very, very much my darling Constance, words will never be able to describe it. Let's do it again someday!!!!!

Thanks, kids, for your love and support."

It has been a very interesting observation for me to read back over my pages to see what progress that I have made in life as I live my "golden years," which have been described by many as golden years that are well tarnished. Yet I feel satisfied with the many exciting and interesting things that I believe I have accomplished to this point. I realize that there are many things left out that perhaps I could have added to my story before closing these years. However, if I lay low on the snack foods, keep allowing my wife to feel that she is the boss, start playing the part of a senior citizen, I may stay around long enough to write a sequel, filling in all the blanks.

Keith and Connie 50 year anniversary.

CPSIA information can be obtained
at www.ICGtesting.com
Printed in the USA
BVHW031607140222
628721BV00002B/6